DE RERUM NATURA
The Poem on Nature

LUCRETIUS (Titus Lucretius Carus) was born *c.* 99 BC. Little is known of his life. St Jerome reports that Lucretius was driven mad by a love potion and that he committed suicide, but there is no evidence for either assertion. He is thought to have died *c.* 55 BC. *De Rerum Natura* was admired by Virgil, but Lucretius was forgotten until the rediscovery of the text at the beginning of the fifteenth century and the publication of the first edition in 1473. Translations of the work were made by John Evelyn and Dryden in the seventeenth century, and it was an important influence on Milton's *Paradise Lost*.

C.H. SISSON was born in 1914. A distinguished poet, translator and novelist he was made a Companion of Honour in 1993 for his services to literature. He is the editor of Edgar Allan Poe's *Poems and Essays on Poetry* in the Fyfield*Books* series.

Fyfield*Books* aim to make available some of the great classics of British and European literature in clear, affordable formats, and to restore often neglected writers to their place in literary tradition.

Fyfield*Books* take their name from the Fyfield elm in Matthew Arnold's 'Scholar Gypsy' and 'Thyrsis'. The tree stood not far from the village where the series was originally devised in 1971.

> *Roam on! The light we sought is shining still.*
> *Dost thou ask proof? Our tree yet crowns the hill,*
> *Our Scholar travels yet the loved hill-side*

from 'Thyrsis'

LUCRETIUS

De Rerum Natura

The Poem on Nature

Translated with an introduction by
C.H. SISSON

FyfieldBooks

CARCANET

First published in Great Britain in 1976 by
Carcanet Press Limited
Alliance House
Cross Street
Manchester M2 7AQ

This impression 2003

A CIP catalogue record for this book is available from the British Library
ISBN 1 85754 723 3

The publisher acknowledges financial assistance from Arts Council England

Printed and bound in England by SRP Ltd, Exeter

CONTENTS

INTRODUCTION

TITUS LUCRETIUS CARUS was born in 99 B.C. or a few years later. He died in 55 B.C. or a few years later than that. What he did in those forty-four years or so, apart from writing his poem, nobody knows.

Nothing is known about his family. It used to be thought that he was one of the upper classes — mainly on the grounds that the degree of literary cultivation he exhibited was not likely to have been found elsewhere. There is a rival view that he was not so well placed socially. It hardly matters, for he was placed wherever he needed to be to gather the material for one of the most extraordinary poems which has come to us from the ancient world. Peter Wiseman has argued (in *Cinna the Poet and Other Roman Essays*, University of Leicester Press, 1974) that where he needed to be was 'a good way from the top' of the social ladder. This argument is supported by a fascinating array of illustrations from the poem. They certainly show that Lucretius was a close and practical observer of the work of several trades, and that his view of the theatre was not from the best seats.

Jerome, towards the end of the fourth century A.D., asserted that Lucretius committed suicide, after having been driven mad by a love potion and writing his poems in lucid intervals. It is the sort of thing which might be expected of a poet. Jerome himself, long after his death, was often painted with a red hat, on the supposition that the Pope must have made so eminent a man a cardinal. There may be no more authority for one story than for the other.

Jerome's second assertion was that Lucretius' poem was edited by Cicero. It is generally supposed that Lucretius admired Cicero, because of some apparent borrowings, in the *De Rerum Natura*, from the orator's version of the Greek poet Aratus. A cynical explanation would be that it was Cicero who inserted the 'borrowings' in Lucretius' poem. It is unlikely that Lucretius was influenced by the inferior work of the distinguished statesman, and not impossible that Cicero might have been willing for people to think that Lucretius was one of his literary disciples.

Lucretius was a slightly younger contemporary of Julius Caesar, and the probable date of his death is about the time when Caesar was invading Britain. At that time Vergil was an adolescent, fifteen or seventeen years old, so the *De Rerum Natura*, published posthumously, came when it would make the most impact. Catullus was perhaps a dozen years younger than Lucretius, and died about the same time. The Memmius to whom Lucretius addressed his poem is thought to have been the same as the one Catullus served in Bithynia — and thought little of, to judge by his XXVIII.

Memmius does not matter much now. He was clearly a patron of some kind, and the idea that he was likely to benefit by philosophical instruction may have been a polite fiction. A question of more interest is what Lucretius meant by invoking Venus at the outset of his poem. His relations with the gods and goddesses were supposed to be so distant as to preclude any hope of help from that quarter. For the declared object of the poem was to relieve people of religious fears. After death there was only annihilation. He did not overtly deny the existence of the gods, but he put them far away in divine abodes where they could not intervene in human affairs, to which they were entirely indifferent. They were indeed of such material that they could not touch us.

This brings us to question what the poem is about. It is generally thought of as an exposition of Epicurean philosophy. In the conventions of the game between poet and patron, that is what Memmius was submitting himself to. There is no doubt of Lucretius' enthusiasm for the task or of his belief in the benefits of the doctrine — saving men in this world by their lack of faith, to borrow a phrase from the very un-Lucretian Marquess of Halifax. Memmius was unlikely to be saved by Epicureanism. He was proceeding through the ordinary public career of an aristocrat in the Roman republic, and for Epicureanism — which was profoundly pessimistic — there was no point in dabbling in such business. But the Epicureanism of Lucretius is not primarily a doctrine about how people should behave. Morality is a boring enough subject and never in itself filled anyone's mind for very long. What Lucretius is concerned with is the explanation of phenomena, which leads to a speculation about the ultimate nature of the universe — a subject which in the long run is more hopeful than conclusive. Lucretius believed passionately in the conclusions of Epicurus,

8

and his passion carries him over the lacunae in his argument.

The argument is roughly this: everything we perceive with our senses comes from something else and, when it changes, turns into something else. Sight, hearing, touch, taste and smell are the sources of all our knowledge. Nothing we know, therefore, can come from nothingness or depart into nothingness. Everything must therefore be made of permanent elements which combine and re-combine in the objects we perceive. The whole universe must be constructed in this way and there can be nothing else. The elements must be too small to be seen, heard, touched, tasted or smelt. But they are material. All phenomena must be explicable by their behaviour. They could not act or move without space to move in. The universe must therefore consist of elements and emptiness. It is infinite and has no centre. Everything changes all the time so the elemental bodies are never still. They are always falling. If they all fell perpendicularly, there would be no combinations. Therefore there must be sometimes slight deviations. When they strike one another, the elemental bodies rebound irregularly. These chance collisions, in an infinite duration, produced everything in the universe. The combinations we see will not last. The elemental bodies continue to fall, the slight deviations continue. In infinite duration every combination occurs and recurs an infinite number of times. There is nothing peculiar about our world or our universe. They are one among an infinite number. Elements continue to rain on them from outside. They will disintegrate like everything else. The movement of elements will continue as before.

Is this the universe we know through science? It is very like a layman's version of it. This has led, in the nineteenth and twentieth centuries, to some misunderstanding of Lucretius. He has been praised as if his merit consisted in his anticipation of the theories of experimental science. He has been patted on the head as if he were a small boy almost as intelligent as we are. It is more interesting to reflect that the ancient world arrived at these notions without the help of experimental science and modern technology, and that such developments have taught us little that is new about fundamental questions. Moreover, since these views were widely held in the ancient world, and Lucretius is merely one of the sources from which we can conveniently learn them, we should look elsewhere for his peculiar contribution to western thought, which was, of course, a poetic contribution.

Because of the expository nature of Lucretius' poem, it is not quite fair to say that it bears the same relationship to the philosophy of Epicurus as *The Divine Comedy* does to medieval theology. But just as the poetic virtue of Dante resides in something not to be found in St. Thomas Aquinas, so the virtue of Lucretius, as a poet, is not to be looked for in an analysis of the doctrine he propounds.

The *De Rerum Natura* is a vision, much as *Piers Plowman* is a vision, though Lucretius is much more powerful as well as more sophisticated. The moments of insight *use* the Epicurean theory as a means of expression, but the vision is of something more terrible than the theory. At the end of Book I, where the argument is against the Stoic doctrine that air and fire are centrifugal, Lucretius sees the walls of the world flying apart, and everything following them out into the void, so that nothing is left

> But emptiness and imperceptible particles.
> For once you admit a place where matter is lacking,
> That place is the gates of death for everything
> And by them the whole creation will make its exit.

It does not matter. poetically, that Lucretius misunderstood this particular Stoic doctrine. What he sees is what matters. Paradoxically, what he sees is the very thing which attracts him to Epicureanism, the horror from which he takes comfort — the eternal rain of invisible, untouchable particles of matter in emptiness into which he will eventually disappear.

If this were all in the *De Rerum Natura,* it would be a bleak book indeed. But the greatness of the poem lies in the tension which exists between this eternity of imperceptibility and emptiness and the brief space of a life in which things can be seen, touched, heard, smelt and tasted. No poem in Latin literature — and few in any literature — could be fuller of impressions of the visible and tangible world. Nature is on dramatic display here.

> Yet when the rivers are swollen by terrible downpours
> Collected on mountain slopes and sent hurtling down,
> They carry before them branches and even whole trees;
> No bridges are strong enough for the sudden onrush,

They crumple; the river, carrying the rain in its arms,
Crashes against the piers and pushes them forward;
They fall with a roar, and they are under the water,
Immense blocks: nothing could stand against the river.
So with the winds . . .

I, ll. 282 ff.

The gentlest things are noted too: the behaviour of lambs, fruit-trees and 'crops of children'. There is an immense amount of direct observation; one is seeing with the eyes of a man in the ancient world when one reads of timber bobbing up when men are trying to hold it down in the water, or of the light falling through the red, yellow and purple of flapping canvas on to the stage and audience in a theatre. These observations come all the more vividly because they are not set descriptive pieces but illustrations in passing of points which Lucretius wants to make in the exposition of his theory.

A great deal of Books V and VI deals with applications of the general physical theory of the Epicureans. The origin and mortality of the world and of the heavenly bodies, the life of primitive man and the beginnings of civilization, thunder, lightning, earthquakes, water-spouts, volcanoes, the magnet — these are among the topics pursued by the curiosity and imagination of the poet. But first, in Book III, he explores the nature of the mind and soul, *animus* and *anima*, which are of course material like the rest of creation — or rather, like the rest of the uncreated universe. They are made of elementary particles and of emptiness, like everything else. The English 'mind' and 'soul' which are used here following the practice of most scholars, and for lack of better equivalents, do not convey precisely what is under discussion. The *animus*, the mind, thinks and to some extent controls the rest of the body; it is situated in the breast and it is the seat of emotion as well as of thought. The *anima*, or soul, is something like a mixture of air and heat, and is spread throughout all the limbs. It goes out in the last breath, but part of it could be lost with the loss of a limb. So it has some dim realtionship with the shades which — wrongly, according to Lucretius — were supposed to wander by the Styx and, in Christian terms, it would be complete at the resurrection of the body.

The elucidation of this theory is accompanied by so much fine observation of the behaviour of living — and dead — bodies that, as so often in Lucretius, the reader may be temporarily persuaded, forgetting that the twentieth century prefers other explanations. Book IV explores sensation and thought in more detail, starting with the 'images' given off by things which are the causes of our perceptions. Food, sleep and dreams are dealt with, and then come two hundred lines or so in which the passion of love is put in its place, with a physical and physiological examination of how best to avoid it, as well as hints on such matters as the position a woman should adopt in intercourse if she wants to conceive. There is little that is not to be found in Lucretius' poem, one way and another.

The poem is usually held to be unfinished. It ends abruptly when, after some more general lines about the nature of disease, Lucretius pours into 150 impassioned lines a description of plague in Athens. Whatever theory scholars may hold as to what should have followed, Lucretius perhaps felt that he could not go beyond this vision of our earthly paradise, where the dead and dying are heaped as at the end of some gigantic tragedy, and men fight over corpses like dogs.

What should have concluded the poem, it is generally thought, is an account of the gods and their dwellings – a subject which in the rest of the poem receives only intermittent and often ironical treatment. Of Lucretius' hatred of the traditional religions of the ancient world there is no doubt. He would have nothing to do with fears and propitiations; early in the poem he pours contempt on the piety of Agamemnon who was ready to sacrifice Iphigenia in Aulis in order to get a favourable wind for his fleet. It is not the gods who are assailed here, but human superstition. Yet if the gods have a formal existence in the universe of Lucretius, they are pared away and consequently as uninteresting to us as, he asserts, we are to them. They did not create the world, they do not intervene in it. They have bodies made of material particles like the rest of us and even sending off images which can visit us in sleep, but are—it is not explained how—immortal. All this is singularly unconvincing, and perhaps inconsistent with the rest of the cosmography. The gods live in a tranquillity which is so complete that it amounts to indifference. According to the Epicurean view, man should live like the indifferent gods.

In fact, this extremely boring and abstract theology accords with only one pole of Lucretius' poetic mind. It is a theology which agrees in tone, if not in logic, with his vision of the

12

universal bleakness outside the world which can be seen and touched. No wonder if, in spite of his warnings, he half believes in the Venus he invokes at the beginning of the poem. For the other pole of his mind is in the sensible world, the world of nature as we know it, and in his apprehension of it the notion of Venus is central. It is less the Venus of pleasure — though there is pleasure in it — than the Venus of a generation repeated again and again in innumerable phenomena. It is not only the animals which copulate. Nothing can come from nothing and one thing is expended in another.

> Nothing indeed is lost of perceptible things.
> One thing is made of another, and nature allows
> No new creation except at the price of a death.
>
> I, ll. 262 ff.

There are oddities in some of Lucretius' explanations, but the impression one gets from an extensive reading of him is far from any antiquarian quaintness. His mind is singularly open and one is very little conscious of the barriers of time. He is engagingly, passionately concerned to set down the truth as he sees it, that 'which we have heard, which we have seen with our eyes, which we have looked upon, and our hands have handled'. He trusts the evidence of the senses. 'If they are not true, then reason itself is a lie'. (IV, l. 485). If he does not see the whole truth, that is a point he has in common with us. Attempts have been made, in Russia and elsewhere, to assimilate Lucretius to Marxism, and in France he was the only Latin poet admitted into a collection entitled *Les Classiques du peuple*.

Dryden has some good remarks on Lucretius, who, he says, 'though often in the wrong, yet seems to deal *bona fide* with his reader, and tells him nothing but what he thinks,' adding that in this 'plain sincerity' he differed from 'our *Hobbs*.' Dryden speaks of the 'perpetual torrent' of Lucretius' verse, though admitting that in some places the subject constrained him, as it does. It was left to Creech to produce the first full English version, in 1674. It must have been found readable at the time, for it went through several editions, but it has lost what immediacy it had. Dryden himself translated some fragments only, including a long passage on the nature of love, from Book IV, of which he says, 'I own it pleas'd me.' The

13

later translations are for the most part the work of men more or less scholarly, more or less impressed by Lucretius' philosophy, but with little gift for English verse and only a mediocre ability to speak plainly in it. Creech apparently continued to serve the eighteenth century. The nineteenth century produced a number of versions, from that of T. Busby in 1813, to the selections turned into the metre of Fitzgerald's *Omar Khayyám* by W. H. Mallock (1900). There was a solid blank verse translation by John Mason Good (Bohn, 1851). Of twentieth-century versions the most elegant is R. C. Trevelyan's (1920-37). There are others, produced on one side or the other of the Atlantic, of which one need only say that they do not provide a reason for anyone else not trying.

The *De Rerum Natura* is one of the great books of the world, and one can only suppose that Ford Madox Ford did not know what he was talking about — as sometimes happened to him, in spite of his immense gifts — when he said, in *The March of Literature*: 'If one were inclined to be severely exclusive, one might permit oneself to refuse [Lucretius] the name of poet altogether.' Ford is not at his happiest in the reasons he gives in support of his opinion. 'It is obvious,' he says, 'that from such subjects nothing which we should normally consider poetry could be evolved. This is not because poetry in itself is unable to confront serious subjects but because poetry consists in the projection of passions, moods or objects and not in their constatation.' To those who have actually read him, Lucretius is more recognizable in Landor's words: 'I admire and love Lucretius. There is about him a simple majesty, a calm and lofty scorn of everything pusillanimous and abject; and, consistently with this character, his poetry is masculine, plain, concentrated and energetic.'

14

BOOK I

The poet invokes Venus, without whom nothing is conceived, and asks his patron Memmius to turn aside from business and listen to his universal explanations. Religious scruples are to be ignored. The gods created nothing; it is obvious that everything comes from something else. Matter consists of solid, permanent and indivisible particles so small as to be below the threshold of perception. Besides them, there is in the universe only emptiness. Everything is made of particles and emptiness, in various arrangements. The poet then examines, with more or less scorn, the rival theories of Heraclitus, Empedocles and Anaxagoras. Finally he explains that the universe, matter and space are all infinite.

Mother of all the Romans: moreover, everyone's pleasure,
Comfortable Venus: everything under the stars
— The sea that carries ships as well as the earth that bears
                                       crops —
Is full of you: every living thing is conceived
By your methods and so comes into the daylight.
The winds elude you and the sky is apt to be cloudless
When your month comes, and under your feet the earth
Sends up her lovely flowers, and the sea's surfaces
Glitter placidly as the light gleams from the sky.

As soon as the face of spring puts in an appearance
And the fertilizing wind blows in from the west
The birds of the air are the first to notice your coming
And your effluence strikes at their very hearts;
The wild cattle jump about in their pastures,
They plunge and swim over the rivers, delight has taken
                                       them.
Then throughout the seas, on the mountains, in hungry
                                       rivers,
In the birds' leafy recesses, on the verdescent plains,
Deep inside every creature appetite stirs
As you provoke them to natural propagation.

Since you alone control the working of nature
Without you nothing can come to these shores of light

And nothing is glad or amiable without you.
I seek your assistance as I write these verses
In which I shall try to explain nature to Memmius,
My friend whom you, Goddess, have always distinguished
With the best gifts which can be found for anyone:
The more, Goddess, endow my words with beauty.
Bring it about meanwhile that military ferocity
On land and sea everywhere falls fast asleep.
It is only you can bring men peace and quiet
For Mars is the one who manages these affairs
And he often throws himself on your belly,
Conquered in turn because desire has wounded him.
He lies there with his handsome neck thrown back,
Gaping at you and feeding on your looks,
His breath hangs on your lips as he falls back.
As he lies there on top of your holy body
Allow your lips to speak gently to him, Goddess.
Ask him, lady, to give the Romans peace
For when the country is going through bad times
I cannot give my mind to my work and Memmius
Cannot resist the temptation to make himself useful.

So, Memmius, give me your undivided attention,
Turn from business and take a look at the truth,
What I am saying I say because I've considered it;
At least don't turn it down till you've understood,
Though it is, indeed, rather a large pretension
To explain all origins, universes, divinities,
To say how nature creates, increases, nourishes,
And how she disposes of bodies when they are done.
I shall call these things material, genetic bodies
Or seminal, if you like, because they are sources,
Or basic matter, as the first matter of all.
Divine nature cannot be other than nature
Subsisting for endless time in an unspoilt peace
Far away from ourselves and the things that touch us;
For deprived of pain, and also deprived of danger,
Able to do what it wants, it does not need us,
Nor understands our deserts, and it cannot be angry.

In the time when people felt the weight of religion,
Wallowing upon the ground and — a ghastly spectacle —

Heaven scowled down upon them and showed no mercy,
A Greek man was the first to raise his eyes,
Daring to look at God and stand against him.
He took no notice at all of the thunder and lightning,
Religious reputations merely incited him;
He said he would expose the secrets of nature
And so, by force of intelligence, and no other,
He pierced beyond the flaming walls of the world,
Paraded up and down the whole immensity
And came back a winner with explanations for everything,
— What could happen, what not, and what were the limits,
All fixed and measured, of every nature and thing.
And so he had religion under his feet.
He won, and as a result we have no superiors.

I fear, at this point, you may be apprehensive
Of possibly getting involved in impious discourse
— As if it were something criminal. I tell you, more often,
It is religion that produces impieties.
Think of what happened at Aulis. They took the girl to
the altar
— The most respectable men in Greece, the convinced top
people —
The blindfold fell from her eyes and she saw her father
Standing there with the executioner priests
Who were trying to keep their carving knives out of *his* sight
And all the bystanders merely blubbered and liked it
Or, dumb with terror, knelt squalidly on the floor.
It did not do the girl any good, at that moment,
That she had seen him as father rather than king.
There were hands enough ready to carry her off to the altar,
Wriggling, but not to the natural rite of a wedding
— An innocent girl betrayed to a sort of incest
To be struck down by the piety of her father
Who hoped in that way to get a good start for his fleet.
That is the sort of horror religion produces.

Maybe some day you will listen to the priests,
Squirm under what they say and leave me standing.
They make so many dreams
To turn aside the reason of your life
And trouble your success with talk of fear.

I understand: if there were some visible end
To human misery, it would be another story,
There would be something to set against the priests.
But as it is there is no chance of resistance,
Nobody understands what the soul is like.
Is it there with the foetus or does it slip in with the
midwife?
Does it die when we do or break itself up in the cemetery?
Or is there some dusky region to which it must go?
Or is it sent to inhabit other cattle?
— As Ennius suggested, and after all he was a poet;
It would not do for me to ignore one of them,
Certainly not one so gifted and famous as he was.
Yet Ennius talks about Acheron and the underworld
As a place where neither souls nor bodies persist
But only shadows of inexplicable pallor.
From these, he says, emerged the picture of Homer
Who began to spill salt tears, by way of preliminary
To explaining to Ennius all the secrets of science.

There is a connection; and if you want to discover
The reason for the movement of heavenly bodies
And, not less important, the laws of what happens on earth,
The first thing must be to attempt to establish
What sort of thing we mean when we talk of a *mind*
And why it happens that everyone is so frightened
In delirium, or even ordinary sleep,
When ghosts pop up, or at least pretend to address us,
In imitation of people we know dead and buried.
It does not escape me that rather obscure Greek systems
Are not the easiest things to put into verse.
I shall have to use a lot of improbable words;
You must put them down to my rather recherché subject.
You must take it all as being a mark of my friendship;
Not everyone would exert himself as I do,
Sitting up late at nights with no other object
Than to try to get a flicker of light in your mind,
Which can only be done by unusual verbal agility
And verse good enough to make you see things as I do
— A matter of having uninterrupted vision,
My dear Memmius, and clarity of reasoning,
So much more reassuring than vulgar daylight.

There is one simple point we have to start from:
The gods never made a single thing out of nothing.
Because, if one thing frightens people, it is
That so much happens, on earth and out in space,
The reasons for which seem somehow to escape them,
And they fill in the gap by putting it down to the gods.
That is why, once we know that nothing can come from
                                                    nothing,
We are on the right track already and likely to see
How everything starts and goes on in an ordered sequence
And nothing at all is merely the work of the gods.

Consider: if things could be made from nothing,
There would be no such thing as the cycle of generation,
You could breed men from the sea, and the land would
                                                    produce
All kinds of fishes and birds, and out of the sky
Herds of cattle come tumbling; wild animals would
Turn up in deserts or farmyards without any reason;
You could not count on an apple-tree giving you apples,
But any sort of tree would produce any fruit.
If everything did not have its seminal elements
How would we ever know what anything comes from?
But, as it is, the origins are determined
And everything comes to the shores of light
The moment its matter has reached the right point of
                                                    development.
No question of undiscriminating creation
When everything has its seeds within itself.

Besides, have you thought why roses come in spring,
Corn ripens in the heat, and the grapes in autumn?
It is because their seeds are so determined
And all creation happens when it must.
It needs only the season, and the vivid earth
As it were finds it safe to produce what it does.
If things came out of nothing, they would come from
                                                    nothing,
Turning up at odd times in a random way;
They would have no natures to hold them to their course
Nor elements answering only to certain seasons.

There would be no question of interval after coition
Before the child appeared, if we came from nothing.
Young men would disconcertingly spring from
                                        perambulators
And full-grown trees appear in a flash from the ground.
As such things do not happen, but on the contrary
Everything grows and changes little by little
And all growth follows the laws of particular species,
It proves that everything's made from its own material.

Added to this is the fact that the annual rainfall
Is one of the things which determines what each place
                                        produces.
Without the appropriate amount there would be no fodder
And that would soon put an end to reproduction.
One might entertain a notion of common elements
— In various combinations, like letters in words —
But not the idea of *no* determining elements.

And then, why is it that nature does not produce giants
To walk across the sea in their seven-league boots
And dig up a mountain or two on their way to the shore?
And why don't people live to extravagant ages
If not because of the limits of the material
Which governs the growth and action of everything?
There is no denying that nothing can come of nothing
When everything has to have seeds, without which no
                                        creature
Could ever find its way to a breath of air.

Finally, why is it cultivated enclosures
Do better than spaces left in their natural state?
It must be that there are some natural elements
Which we, by turning up the productive furrows
And cutting in with the plough, somehow release.
If none of these things was true, we should not need to work
And nature indeed would get on better without us.

Another point: nature breaks things down to their elements
But never proceeds to the stage where there is *nothing*:
For if there were things of which all the parts were
                                        destructible

20

They would suddenly disappear before our eyes;
No effort would be required to break up an object
For only permanent elements hold things together.
As it is, since everything has its permanent elements
Until something hits it, or gets into its interstices
And so destroys or explodes its presented nature,
Nothing is ever allowed to come to an end.

Besides, if all the things time removes from our sight
Were really destroyed and all their matter consumed,
How would the animal world be saved from destruction,
As generation does save it? Or how would the earth
Have ingenuity to continue to feed it?
How would the sea get fed by the springs and rivers?
Or how would the sky find food for its flocks of stars?
None of these things would happen, if mortal bodies
Had been consumed by time in the infinite past.
But if, in the space of past and the time gone by,
There have always been elements ready for re-confection,
They are by nature immortal, that is certain
And that is why they cannot return to nothing.

All objects would be destroyed by a single cause
If there were not eternal matter to hold them together
More or less tightly, in various patterns or systems.
A touch would be enough to produce destruction.
If things were not composed of permanent elements
Any force would at once unravel the pattern.
As it is, patterns hold together in various ways
But substance is always identical and eternal
And so things hold until a force is encountered
Which is just enough to rip their particular texture.
So you see once more that nothing returns to nothing:
What happens is that things revert to their common elements.

The rains are gone, when the upper air has thrown them
Into the lap of our darling mother the Earth
But the shining harvests come, the branches turn green,
The trees grow upwards, then are borne down by the fruit
And so our race is fed, and the animals too;
The happy cities flower with their crops of children,
The leafy woods sing out with the new year's birds;

21

So the well-fleshed herds sink down in the happy grass
And the udders swell to bursting with each day's milk;
So the lambs are driven to dance on their tottering legs
And play as if mothers' milk had turned their brains.
Nothing indeed is lost of perceptible things.
One thing is made of another, and nature allows
No new creation except at the price of death.

You know I have said creation out of nothing
Is nonsense. So is destruction of things to nothingness.
But since you may doubt the validity of a doctrine
Requiring the existence of invisible elements,
I should like to draw your attention to certain bodies
Which must be allowed to exist, although we can't see them.

Think of the winds, which beat up the sea with their blows,
Wrecking the largest vessels, scattering the clouds;
And sometimes, driving a hurricane over the plains,
Strewing great trees on the ground, and with shattering
                                                    blasts
Lashing the mountaintops: a roaring, a fury,
There is rage to come in their smallest menacing murmur.
No doubt at all, the winds are invisible bodies
Which sweep across the sea, the earth and the sky
And toss the clouds and carry them off in a storm.
You may compare them and the damage they do
To what is done by water, whose nature is gentle,
Yet when the rivers are swollen by terrible downpours
Collected on mountain slopes and sent hurtling down,
They carry before them branches and even whole trees;
No bridges are strong enough for the sudden onrush,
They crumple; the river, carrying the rains in its arms,
Crashes against the piers and pushes them forward;
They fall with a roar, and they are under the water,
Immense blocks: nothing could stand against the river.
So with the winds; it must be, their action is similar
For like a river they lash wherever they choose,
Pushing whatever impedes them, overturning
In one or several assaults; sometimes they lift
And carry things upwards in an eddying swirl.
It proves, it must prove, that winds are invisible bodies,

For by their action and habit they rival the rivers
Which no one denies are made of a visible substance.

Or again, take smell. We perceive all manner of odours
But never observe one on its way to our noses.
Nor does sight communicate blazing heat or cold weather
Or enable us to detect or distinguish a sound;
Yet the nature of all these things must of course be physical
Since otherwise they could not impress our senses
— For impression means touch, and touch means the touch
                                             of bodies.

Then observe, if you hang clothes out where the waves
                                        are breaking,
They get wet, just as they dry if they're spread in the sun.
Yet nobody ever saw how the damp gets into them
Or how it gets out when the weather is hot.
It follows that moisture must be composed of particles
So small it is not possible they should be seen.
In the same way, if you wear a ring on your finger,
After many years it will wear perceptibly thin;
A drip will hollow a stone; the blade of a plough
In time will secretly wear away in the fields;
And paving-stones grow smooth and thin with crowds
Who tread on them year by year: by a city gate
You may see a statue of bronze with the right hand worn
Where travellers have kissed it as they went on their way.
These things diminish, we see, by little and little,
But what is lost at any particular time
Is something that nature does not allow us to see
Any more than she allows us to see what is added
To bodies in the course of their natural growth.
The same is true of what is taken away
From bodies when they are wasted by time and age;
And there are half-eaten cliffs overhanging the sea,
But who ever saw the salt removing a mouthful?
Nature does all these things with invisible substances.

Not everywhere, however, is crowded with matter,
For nature is such that everything has its emptiness.
This is a necessary part of the lesson,
Without which nature would continue to mystify you

And my theories of it would in fact be incomplete.
There is the emptiness of unoccupied space,
Without which, clearly, nothing could ever move.
The function of matter is to get in the way;
If there were no space nothing could ever move
But everything get in the way of everything else.
Nothing would ever give, and nothing would budge.
But in fact we see the seas move, the earth, the clouds,
The stars sweep by, and everything has its movement.
If there were no emptiness none of this could happen,
Nothing indeed could ever change or begin;
There would be close-packed matter and that would be all.

The fact is, things which appear to us to be solid
Are really made of somewhat rarified stuff.
That is why water drips through the roof of a cave
And it looks as if thick slabs of rock had burst into tears;
That is why food distributes itself through the body:
Trees grow, and manage in time to produce their fruit
Because what they feed on is carried from roots to the trunk
And so in the end to the very tip of the branches.
Noises don't stop at a wall but are carried right through,
It makes no difference that the house is shut up;
The cold gets into our bones: and none of these things
Could happen, unless there were spaces matter could get
                                                              through.

And why is it some things weigh a lot more than others
Although the volume is exactly the same?
A lump of bread and a lump of wool, for example?
The difference must be in the proportion of matter.
The nature of matter is to press everything down
While the nature of empty space is to be without weight.
It follows that, with objects of equal volume,
The lighter must be the one which contains more space
And the heavier must be the one which contains more matter
While the space it contains must be accordingly smaller.
This demonstrates that the composition of things
Includes, as well as matter, some empty space.

Here I must warn you against a plausible theory
Which some people have advanced, and which might
                                                              mislead you.

Its proponents say that water gives way to the fish
As it swims, and opens a passage for it to pass,
Because there is a space left behind the fish
Into which the liquid can flow: and this, they say,
                                        demonstrates
How other things can change place, although space is full.
This explanation rests on erroneous reasoning,
For how after all can the fish find a way to move forward
If the water does not give way to it? And how can the water
Give way to the fish, unless the fish can move forward?
For either one has to deny that bodies can move
Or else admit they contain an empty element
Which makes it possible for movement to begin.

And then, if two flat objects are brought together
And at once rebound, the space that is made between them
Is filled up with air, but, however quickly the air moves,
It cannot fill up the whole space instantaneously:
The process of filling, though rapid, happens by stages.

If anyone should maintain, when the two bodies separate,
That condensation of air is what makes it possible,
He is wrong: for that would mean a vacuum created
Where there wasn't one before, while the vacuum which
                                        did exist
Had somehow been filled up. Air cannot condense
In such a manner, I think, or if it were possible,
It would not be without the existence of space
In the air itself, into which its parts could withdraw
— So though you might hesitate at these objections,
You would have to admit that empty space does exist.

I could go on adding to the arguments I have adduced
If I felt I had to scrape together a proof,
But the indications I have given are enough
For so intelligent a reader as yourself.
Just as the dogs, merely by using their noses,
Succeed in finding their quarry under a fern
Once they have got the scent and can follow it up;
So you can find one consequence after another
In an inquiry like this, like following a thread
Through every obscurity until you light on the truth.

Of course if you choose to dawdle or stray from the scent,
My dear Memmius, you can't expect very much.
But here I am, gulping the stuff from the fountain
And willing to let it trickle out of my mouth;
My only fear is that age will come up behind us
And, with its scissors, snip our nervous connections,
Before I can bring my metrical explanation
To any completeness at all on any one point
Let alone give you the full weight of the argument.

But now I must get back to what I was saying.
The whole of nature consists of two elements:
There are material bodies, and there is empty space,
In which they are situated and through which they move.
The existence of material bodies is plain to the senses;
If we were not sure of that self-evident starting-point
We would have no basis for more abstruse constructions.
For all proof rests in the end on a basis of sense.
As for place, or space, or if you will call it emptiness,
We know that this is there because, if it were not, bodies
Could not be anywhere, nor would they be able to move,
A point I demonstrated a few lines back.

There is indeed nothing whatever of which you can say
That it exists apart from matter and emptiness,
As if there were some third element in the universe.
For if there were, it would not exist without size
— How large or small, is a matter of indifference —
And if it were sensible, even to the lightest touch
It would be classified with material objects;
If it could not be touched it would be incapable
Of offering the slightest resistence to any body,
Which amounts to saying that it would be empty space.

Besides, if a thing exists it must either act
Or else be acted upon by other agents,
Or provide a space in which other things can exist.
But only material objects can act and be acted on,
And only empty space can provide a space.
Apart from emptiness and material objects
There can be no third element in nature
— No third which could have an effect on our senses
Or be the subject of any reasoning.

You will find that everything which can be named
Is either inherent in the two basic elements
Or is the effect of something that happens to them.
The inherent qualities are those which cannot be separated
Without destroying the nature of the object;
As weight in rocks, heat in fire, and wetness in water,
Or tangibility in material objects
And in space — or emptiness — intangibility.
On the other hand, servitude, poverty and riches,
Liberty, war, and settlements, and so on,
Which leave material bodies unchanged in their nature
Are things which happen to bodies — we might say, events.

Time has no existence by itself
And it is only from the perception of things
Past, present and future that the mind is aware of it.
There never was anyone had even a glimpse of time
Apart from the movement of things and the contrast of rest.

So it is absurd to suggest that the Trojan War
Or the rape of Helen, has some sort of real existence
When the ages in which these notable things occurred,
Like the people they happened to, have been swept away.
Whatever happened is no more than just a happening
— Other places or times, perhaps, it makes no difference.

For if there had been no matter to form the bodies
And no empty space in which they could perform,
Paris would not have been there to get excited
Nor Helen in such a shape as to set him on
And the famous wars would not have happened at all.
No wooden horse could have turned out a load of Greeks
Into the darkness, to set the town alight.
You can see from that, all that has gone on in the past
Has no existence, as matter and empty space have,
But rather should be regarded as so many happenings
Which have occurred to material bodies in space.

The bodies themselves are of two kinds: the particles
And complex bodies constructed of many of these;
Which particles are of an invincible hardness
So that no force can alter them or extinguish them.

27

It is not easy to imagine a body
So full of itself as to be entirely solid:
For lightning travels with ease through the walls of houses
And so do all kinds of sound; iron glows in the fire
And even stones break up in a violent heat;
Gold which seems hard enough can grow liquid too,
And so can bronze, which falls like a block of ice;
Warmth goes through silver, and so indeed does the cold
So that when we hold a silver cup in our hands
We feel the iced wine rise as it is poured.
Enough to convince us that nothing is really solid.

In fact, if one thinks about it and looks at the evidence,
It turns out, as I'll explain in a very few verses,
That there are things made of solid and changeless matter
Which are the basic constituents of the universe
From which all comes and without which nothing is made.

First of all, since it is clear that nature is twofold,
Consisting of elements of quite different kinds,
Body, and space in which all events take place,
These two must be quite separate from each other.
For where there is space with nothing in it but emptiness,
There can be no body there; and where there is body,
It clearly will not do to talk about emptiness.
So particles are quite solid and have no space in them.

Since there is emptiness in created things,
It must be surrounded by something solid:
For could things hide such emptiness in their interior
If there were no material around to hide it?
And what could this be except a collection of particles
Arranged to form a sort of screen for the void?
Matter, consisting entirely of solid particles,
Can be eternal, though everything made of it dies.

Then, if there were no such thing as empty space,
Everything would be solid; on the other hand,
If there were not bodies which filled up all the space
They occupied, so that nothing else could intrude,
The universe would be nothing but emptiness.
But matter and space, in fact, are alternatives,

They cannot be both in one place; the world is neither
Made up entirely of the one nor of the other
And this mixed nature of things would only be possible
If there were bodies which did not give way to the void.

These bodies — the particles — cannot break up at a blow,
Nor can anything get past their outer defences,
Nor can they yield or give way whatever may come
— All these are points that I have already made.
It is evident, therefore, that but for the empty space,
Nothing could crash or break or be split in two,
Nor even get soaked, or penetrated by cold,
Nor even eaten by fire, the general destroyer.
The more unoccupied space each object contains,
The more it will give way to the things which destroy it.

Besides, it is clear, if matter had not been eternal,
Before now everything would have returned to nothing
And everything we now see would have come from nothing.
But I have already proved that nothing can be created
From nothing, nor anything created return to nothing.
There must therefore be immortal elements
Into which all things in time can be dissolved
And from which all things can be renewed once again.
These elements must be of a solid simplicity
For how, otherwise, could they last through so many ages
And take part endlessly in the renewal of things?

And how, if nature had not provided some end
To the destruction of things, could matter have held
Against the breaking up through so many ages,
Or how could things be conceived and brought to maturity
In any measure of years, and last out their time?
For everything that we see is more easily broken
Than put together again: the procession of days
And endless duration of all the time gone by
Would surely have broken up everything, crushed and
                                            dissolved it,
So that nothing could be re-made in the time that remains.
But some end to destruction indeed has been fixed,
For do we not see that everything is renewed?
And definite times fixed for the life of everything,
And everything in due time arrives at its flower?

This too: although you have the most solid material
In the basic particles, yet that can easily give you
The soft and fluid: as air, earth, water and mist.
How they are formed and behave is easy to see
Once the existence of empty space is admitted,
But if you imagined the basic ingredients were soft,
How could you ever arrive at iron or flint?
You could not explain them: there would not be in all nature
The qualities out of which such stuff could be made.
So then: it is the strength of solid simplicity
Lies at the root of creation; the more or less density
Of basic particles makes up the strength of each object.

Since the limits of growth and living for every species
Are fixed as if by an immutable law,
Which also defines what they can and cannot do
And nothing is ever changed: but so fixed indeed
That all the different birds in a perfect order
Show their unchangeable markings according to species;
Could these things happen without immutable matter?
For if the original particles were not stable
But liable to give way to modifications,
How could it be so determined what things are born?
Or how could there be the certain limits there are
To what each species can do and the turn of its nature?
And how could the generations bring back as they do
The character, movements and habits of those before them?

The original particles, although themselves invisible,
Must have limits, which means, a series of points
And these must be the smallest bodies in nature,
Without parts; points moreover which never existed
In isolation, or could so ever exist
Since they are only parts of another body
— Units which, joined together with others like them,
Make up the bodies of the original particles.
And since these points have no existence apart,
They must remain eternally glued together.
So the particles are of solid and simple nature,
Made up of crowded irreducible points
And not the product of any act of assembly,
But such that they have always existed in that conjunction:

No kind of separation or any subtraction
From the particles which are the seeds of everything.

For if there were no such thing as a minimal entity,
The smallest bodies would have infinite parts;
There would be no end to the foolish arithmetic
Of dividing by half, by half and by half again.
And in that case there would be no difference of size
Between the smallest thing and the infinite universe,
Because however large you supposed the latter
The former, like it, would be made up of infinite parts.
This is something that reason simply cannot accept,
And the mind has no alternative but to admit
The existence of parts which cannot be further divided
— The minimal natural entities, finite points.
And since they exist, they must be solid and changeless.

One may add, that if it had been the habit of nature
To reduce things to their irreducible parts,
Nothing could ever again have been made from them;
For things which have not the benefit of any parts
Would not have the qualities of productive matter
— The power of interaction and the movement which are
The normal ways in which things ever happen.

Those who imagine that fire is the basic substance
And that everything else in the world is made from that
Seem to me to have taken leave of their senses.
Heraclitus was first to parade this absurd opinion
And he was greatly esteemed for his obscurity,
Though not among those who wanted to find out the truth.
Fools have a preference for secrets in intricate language
And you might say their way of detecting the truth
Is to try a favoured formula out on their ear-drums
And if it sounds musical, that is enough for them.

For how, I ask you, could there be such variety,
If everything came purely and simply from fire?
It would make no difference that fire could become more
                                              rarified,
Or denser, so long as its nature remained unchanged.
No doubt it would be hotter where it was more concentrated

And less so where its elements were dispersed;
I do not see you could draw other inferences
From such a starting-point, and much less explain
How all the variety that is found in nature
Could come from the expansion and contraction of fire.

There is this too: only if the existence of emptiness
Is admitted, does expansion and contraction make sense,
But those who propose this theory find that unacceptable
Because it weakens their theory at other points,
And they would rather be wrong than face up to the
                                                    difficulties;
Nor do they see that once you leave emptiness out
The whole of creation becomes a single entity,
Densely packed and not conceivably capable
Of sending out light and heat in the way that fire does:
Which shows that fire is not a compacted substance.

Perhaps they are entertaining another hypothesis,
That fires come together, go out and so change their bodies
But if they hold to that without qualification
They are in effect asserting that fire is destructible
And that, in the end, things are re-created from nothing.
For anything which departs from its proper limits
Must be regarded as having ceased to exist,
But some elemental fire must be left untouched
Or once again you are driven back upon nothing
And asserting the whole of creation springs from that.

In fact, there are certain bodies which keep their nature
Without variation, and by their coming and going
And changes of order, produce all natural variety;
But certainly these are not composed of fire.
For how could the coming and going make any difference,
The changing of places and the changing of order
If all the time they kept the nature of fire?

The truth of the matter is this: there are certain particles
Whose coming together, movement, position and so on
Makes fire, and which, as soon as their order is altered
Form into different things: they are not like fire,
Nor are they indeed, one may say, like anything else

Which has the power of striking upon our senses
By sending out particles or else, directly, by contact.
To say that fire is everything, with Heraclitus,
And that nothing else in the world has a real existence,
Is really a form of philosophical madness.
It literally means you have taken leave of your senses,
On which we depend, after all, for all our evidence
— As Heraclitus did for his knowledge of fire.
He thinks indeed we can know fire through the senses,
But not the rest of creation, however brilliant:
That surely is an idiotic distinction.
Where then shall we go for evidence if not to the senses?
By what other means shall we know the true from the false?

And why on earth should Heraclitus abolish
Everything except fire, and let that stand?
Why not abolish fire and leave all the rest?
Both opinions seem to me equally imbecile.

That is why those who think fire is the basic element
And say that everything could be made up of that;
And those who attribute creation rather to air;
And those who consider water the true creator,
Or think that earth is the matter and maker of everything
Seem to me to be wandering away from the facts.
You might say the same of those who prefer two elements,
As fire and water together, or earth and water;
And those who think everything could be made from four
And so lump fire, earth, air and water together.

The chief exponent of this view is Empedocles,
The philosopher who was born in the three-cornered island
Round which the seas run into inlets and bays,
Splashing the green waves to innumerable drops.
Here is the narrow sea with the hurried current
Which flows between the Italian coast and Sicily.
Here is the hungry Charybdis, and here is Etna,
Murmuring and threatening again to gather its anger
Until it vomits fire from its sickened jaws
And fills the sky with lightning of its flames.
Although this seems a great and wonderful land,
Deserving admiration — or even a visit —

Bursting with wealth and able to turn out an army,
Nothing that it has produced can equal Empedocles,
Call him a saint, or a wonder, or merely a treasure.
The poetry that he emitted still re-echoes —
No wonder, for it contains so many discoveries
You would hardly think him human enough for literature.
And yet this man, like the others we have been speaking of,
— Admittedly he was much the best of the bunch —
Although distinguished by remarkable insight,
The author of many impeccable pronouncements,
And certainly more reliable than the priestess
Perched on a tripod and speaking for Apollo:
When he got to first principles he made a mess of it,
All the more, you may say, for being intelligent.

First, he didn't see movement must imply emptiness;
And likewise supposed that soft and rarified bodies,
Air, sun, fire, earth, animals, vegetation,
Could all exist without having empty space in them.

And then he spoke as if matter were so divisible
That you could go on chopping it up to infinity
And hadn't to stop, as you have, at some smallest point:
While in fact we know that everything has its limits
— Speaking first of the things the senses can notice —
And we can conclude from that that the bodies we can't see
Have limits consisting of irreducible points.

Besides, those who insist that the basic elements
Are made of soft matter, should reflect that such things
                                        are perishable;
A universe made of them would certainly die
And everything, once again, would be born from nothing:
Which we have already agreed is impossible.
Moreover, elements of that kind would be poison
To one another: when they came together, they'd die,
Or they would scatter, as we see happen with storm-clouds
Which are dissipated in lightning, wind and rain.

If everything were to be formed of the four elements
And everything again disolve into them,
Why should you think that things are made of the elements

And not the other way round, elements of other things?
There would in fact be a sort of mutual creation
And endless interchange of colours and natures.

Or perhaps you think that the elements join together
Without any change in their respective natures,
Air, earth, water, fire, retaining their characteristics:
If that were the case, nothing could be made from them,
No living creature, or even a thing like a tree,
For each of the elements would display its own nature;
You would see air mixed with earth, or fire mixed with
                                                    water,
As plainly as if they were still separate things.
True elements surely must be of such a nature
As cannot be known directly to the senses
Lest anything should stand out and deprive the object
Of what should be its proper character.

Some theorists trace all back to a heavenly fire
And first suppose that fire turns into air
And then that air converts itself to water
And after that that water changes to earth,
The process then being repeated in reverse
— Earth, water, air, and so back to fire again:
And so the elements go on changing for ever,
Wandering from sky to earth, from earth to the stars,
In a manner quite unbecoming for primary elements:
There has to be something left which is immutable
If the whole creation is not to come to nothing.
For anything to depart from its proper limits
Is literally death to whatever it was before.
It must be therefore that the four natural elements,
Forever changing about among themselves,
Are made of something else which refuses to change,
For otherwise you would have everything back to nothing.
Isn't it better therefore to suppose there are basic particles
Of such a nature that they can, for example, form fire,
And then, by losing or gaining a few of their number
And making some change in their movements or disposition,
Form air? That would account for all natural changes.

You may say that it is obvious everything grows
Into the air and out of the earth which nourishes it,

And that it is only because the rain comes pouring
Down in due season, enough to shake all the trees,
And the sun in its turn blazes and brings its warmth,
That harvests and trees and animals can grow.

Of course: and indeed unless we get food and moisture
Our bodies waste away, and life at last
Springs out of nerves and bones and disappears.
It is true enough that we need certain things to nourish us
And other creatures need other things as we know:
It is because so many particles are combined
In so many ways in all the creatures there are
That different things have need of such different
                                    nourishments.
And it is significant just what the mixture is,
As well as how the particles are arranged
And what the pattern of movement is among them.
For the particles are the same in sky, sea, rivers,
Earth, sun, all crops, all trees, all living things,
But in different patterns and moving in different ways.
It is not so different as you might think with verses,
For so many letters are common to so many words,
Yet the words and verses differ from one another
And that is true of meaning as well as sound.
And this is only a change in the order of elements;
The variations for particles are more numerous
And so make all the variations of nature.

Now let us have a look at Anaxagoras
Whose theory goes by the name of homoeomeria,
For which there is no suitable expression in English
Though the thing itself is easy enough to explain.
For what he means by his homoeomeria
Is that bones are made up of tiny pieces of bone,
Flesh is made up of tiny pieces of flesh,
Blood by the confluence of millions of drops of blood.
He thinks that lots of grains of gold will indeed make gold
And that earth is composed of lots of bits of earth,
That fire is made out of fires, and water from water:
And everything else is made in a similar manner.

He does not, however, admit the existence of emptiness
Nor think there is any limit to sub-divisions.

In both these matters he seems to me on the same footing
As those whose theories I have already discussed.

The elements that he relies on are too feeble,
If you can call them elements, since their nature
Is the same as that of all the things we can see;
They operate and die like everything else.
Which of them could hold back on the slippery slope
And escape from death, when its teeth are in their neck?
Fire? or water? or air? Which of them? Blood or bone?
Nothing, I think: for all things equally die,
Just as the things we see with our eyes
Die in the face of some invincible force.
But nothing that vanishes can be turned to nothing,
Nor things grow out of nothing; this I have proved.

Again, since the body grows with the food we eat
It can be concluded that veins, and blood and bones
And nerves are made of matter which is unlike them:
Or if the contention is that all food is composite,
Containing tiny packets of nerves and bones,
To say nothing of bits of veins and dollops of blood,
Then you have to say that all food and drink is composed
Of matter which bears no resemblance to food and drink,
In fact of bones, nerves and serum, all mixed up with blood.

And if everything which shoots up out of the earth
Is in the earth to begin with, the earth must be
Made up of the heterogeneous things which come out of it.
Apply this argument to whatever you like:
If flame and smoke and ash are hidden in wood
The wood must consist of things unlike itself.

This leaves one way of getting out of the difficulty,
And Anaxagoras takes it; he contends
That every kind of thing is concealed in everything
While the thing we see is simply the one which predominates
Or has somehow come to the surface of the mixture;
But that opinion seems to me far from sensible.
For if it were true you might expect that corn
As it was ground in the mill would sometimes show traces
of blood

37

Or other components of the body it is to feed.
Likewise when we pound up herbs, blood would ooze out;
And you might expect the water drunk by the sheep
To taste a bit like the milk which comes from their udders;
Indeed you might expect, when soil is turned up,
To find in it traces of corn and all kinds of plants
Which are supposed to be concealed there in miniature;
So ash and smoke, you might think, would be found in wood
When you break it up, and tiny pieces of fire.
As none of these things appears it is fair to conclude
That things are not mixed up with each other like that,
But that the particles, mixed in various ways,
Are all the same and common to many things.

You may say that in the forests which cover the mountains
It often happens that, under the stress of great winds,
The branches of neighbouring trees will rub together
And suddenly fire break out like a monstrous flower:
Yes, quite: but that doesn't mean there is fire in timber;
It simply means there are inflammable elements
Which rubbing together will bring into closer contact,
And this is enough to set the forest on fire.
If the wood in fact contained a ready-made flame,
It would never be possible to conceal the fire;
The forests would all burn up and the trees disappear.

Now perhaps you will see — as I have already explained it —
Why it matters so much how the particles lie,
In what position, or how they push one another?
With very small changes the identical particles
Make wood or fire, just as, you may say, the same letters
— Or almost the same — will produce the words *fir* or *fire*,
With different sounds and certainly different meanings.

Indeed, if you take the view that the visible universe
Cannot be created without recourse to elements
Which have the nature of sensible things themselves,
You might as well give up all idea of elements.
You will find yourself next with particles shaking with
                                                    laughter
Or others standing by with tears in their eyes.

Better listen instead to what I have to say.
I am not under any illusion that it is easy
But I have the support of my passion for reputation,
I can even claim a certain addiction to poetry
And — what does not always go with it — some mental
                                        energy.

Thus equipped, I am not afraid of unpromising country;
I reckon to find enough springs and pick enough flowers,'
And if I achieve anything it will be on a subject
Which has not been a favourite with poets before:
And any subject which matters is rather unusual.
Mine is to extricate the mind from religion.
Moreover, in writing on this difficult subject,
I aim at lucid and even agreeable verse,
And that should not be considered a superfluity.
It is rather as doctors, when they want to give children
Some nasty medicine, give it a flavour of honey
Which is held to be a legitimate trick upon innocence
And persuades the children—perhaps—to swallow the stuff.
Some doctors even claim that the children get better.

So I, since what I have to say is unpleasant
To people who haven't given the subject a thought,
And can produce a revulsion in ordinary men,
Attempt to give it a touch of aesthetic coating
And hope you may recognize sweetness when you taste it:
If I can hold your attention by such devices
So that you read to the end, you will find you have
                                        swallowed
My whole account, so to speak, of the nature of nature.

My theory is that bodies of solid matter
— Particles — move through the ages and are indestructible.
The question now is: are they of limited number?
And is place, emptiness, space, in which everything must
                                        happen,
Finite itself, or does it stretch out without limit
In all directions without any end at all?

The universe is in fact without limit of any kind,
For if it had it would have to have an outside.
Nothing can have an outside unless there is something
                                        beyond it

So the point can be seen at which it ceases to be
And beyond which the senses could not follow it.
There can be no such point for the whole creation;
If one thinks of the whole there can be nothing outside it,
It can have no limit or measure, you could not conceive it.
It does not matter what position you occupy,
Space must stretch an infinite distance in every direction.

Let us suppose for a moment that space is finite;
Then let someone proceed to the furthest boundaries
And throw a spear beyond the point where he is.
You then have to choose whether you think it will travel
In the direction he sends it, as far as you like,
Or whether you think that something will get in the way.
With neither answer can you avoid the conclusion
That the universe stretches out on all sides for ever,
For whether the spear finds something in the way
And cannot proceed, or whether the way is open,
The point it started from is not the end of the universe.
In this manner one can go on, and you put the limit
Wherever you will, I say: Now, where is the spear?
There is no point at which you can set a boundary;
The more space you give the spear, the further it goes.

If indeed the sum of total existing space
Were bounded in fact by limits on every side,
Matter would then fall down and lie on the floor of the
                                                universe
And this indeed would have happened long ago
And there would have been no events at all after that.
There would not even be sky, or the light of the sun
For all the matter there is would stay piled up
In a heap produced by endless ages of sinking.
However, as things are, the particles have no rest
And we may be sure there is no bottom of things
On which they could settle down and take their rest.
Always and everywhere, there is ceaseless motion,
As hurtling particles of eternal matter
Supply what is needed out of infinite space.

Lastly, we see with our eyes how one thing defines another,
How hills are divided by air, and the air by mountains,

How the land marks off the sea, and the sea marks off all
                                                    the land:
There is nothing at all to limit the universe.
It is the nature of space in its farthest depths
That a flash of lightning could travel through it for ever
Yet, as it glided over the endless track,
Never reach a point where the distance before it was less.
So more than huge indeed is the total of things,
Having no limit, and stretching in every direction.

Nature herself makes sure that there is no end to the universe
For she has provided that matter should end in space
And that space can exist only where bounded by matter,
And that the two in turn should make up the universe;
Or, if one of them did not limit the other,
It would itself stretch out without any end;
There would be no sea, no earth, no fabulous sky,
No human race, nor the sacred bodies of gods,
Not for a single moment could they subsist,
For matter, forced out of its patterns, would fall to its
                                                    elements
And so be carried away into the void;
Or rather nothing would ever have been created
For nothing could bring the scattered parts together.

It was certainly not by design that the particles fell into
                                                    order,
No trace there of an intelligent mind;
They did not work out what they were going to do,
But because many of them by many chances
Struck one another in the course of infinite time
And encountered every posssible form and movement,
They found at last the disposition they have,
And that is how the universe was created:
So particles, kept together for so many years,
When by a chance they had found harmonious movements,
Brought it about that rivers flow into the sea
To keep it going, while earth by the heat of the sun
Renews its products, and living creatures breed on
And the gliding lights in the sky are never put out.
Certainly none of these things could do as they do
If there were not an infinite store of matter

From which they could make up their losses whenever
                                                    they need.
For just as an animal cannot live without food
Since his flesh will waste away; so it is with all things
Which must replenish their matter or disappear.

Blows raining on any world from the outside
Cannot entirely suffice to keep it together.
They can often manage to keep it partly in check
While other particles come to make up the whole.
At times, however, they bounce back from the contact
And then some matter from the original whole
May make its escape from that particular system
And so again more particles are required.
Indeed there must, for the bombardment itself,
Be an infinite store of matter in every direction.

Memmius, do not believe those who maintain
That everything tends to the centre of the universe
And that the world is such that it holds its own
Without the need for any external bombardment;
That the upper and lower ends are held by central attraction
(How could you believe that anything rests in itself?);
That bodies on the lower side of the earth
All press upwards and are at rest on the ground
As if they were the reflections we see in water:
Those who defend such notions also maintain
That animals in those parts walk upside-down,
No more falling into the sky down below them
Than we fly into the sky that is above us:
And that they see the sun when we see the stars,
In fact the other half of the sky which we do not see,
And that their days are equivalent to our nights.

That is the sort of position fools get into
Through having embraced such idiotic principles.
How could an infinite universe have a middle?
Or if it did have, why should anything stop there
Rather than at some other point in the universe?
Is it not obvious that place or space or emptiness,
Whether you're talking about the middle or not,
Must give way to heavy bodies, from any direction?

There is no place where bodies can come and find
They have lost their weight and can stand still in the void;
Nor can any emptiness offer resistance,
Its nature is such that it must always give way.
It cannot therefore be that what holds things together
Is the imagined attraction which lies at the core.

Those who say such things do not assert that all bodies
Seek the centre, but those made of water and earth,
The sea, for example, the torrents which come from the
                                                    mountains,
And other things of terrestial constitution.
They hold on the other hand that aerial breezes
And burning fires attempt to escape from the middle,
So that the explanation of stellar twinklings
And of the great sun eating up the sky
Is that bits of fire from the middle have got stuck there;
And they assert that leaves could not grow on treetops
If they were not fed by food pressing up from the ground
        .   .   .   .

Lest, with the wings of flame, the walls of the world
Should fly apart and be suddenly lost in the void
And everything follow them out for a similar reason;
The haunts of thunder would suddenly be swept upwards
And under our feet the whole earth would give way
So that everything disappears in confusion and ruin,
Crumbling to particles and streaming out into space
And in a moment of time there would be nothing left
But emptiness and imperceptible particles.
For once you admit a place where matter is lacking,
That place is the gates of death for everything
And by them the whole creation will make its exit.

If you learn these things, which requires no great labour,
Since one thing follows quite simply from another,
You will not stumble, nor the secrets of nature
Be dark to you. One thing lights up another.

43

BOOK II

The poet expatiates on the pleasures of being a philosopher, and looking down on the world at large. He explains the movement of the basic particles of matter, how they fall through space and are occasionally and irregularly deflected. Then he describes the various shapes of the elemental bodies, and their effects on us. In various combinations they make heaven and earth, trees, ourselves — everything. As those combinations change, the things they constitute change. They grow as they assimilate more elements from the infinite supply and decline as they lose more. Everything has its youth, maturity and death.

It is pleasant enough to see other people in trouble;
The shore is an excellent place for watching a shipwreck:
Not that one enjoys the cries of the drowning,
But it is reassuring not to be drowning oneself.
Just so, one may find a battle quite agreeable
So long as one's own position is clearly quite safe:
But most delicious of all is to be a philosopher,
Perched on an edifice constructed by the wise,
From which you can look down on people, and see them
Wandering around the world like so many sheep
— If sheep may try to be clever, be proud of their ancestry,
Or spend their days and nights in a state of exacerbation
. Because they are trying to be rich or have some success in
                                           politics.

The qualities needed are blindness and mental debility
If one is to delight in living in crises
What little one lives at all. Can people not see
Our nature has no needs except to be quiet,
The body to be completely exempt from pain
And the mind enjoying a freedom from fear and care?

What little is required for physical happiness
Is just enough to remove any source of pain
For that of itself will be enough for pleasure;
Our nature does not indeed demand any more.
Naked statues are not at all indispensable

As a means of holding up the illuminations;
Some simpler arrangement will quite well see you through
                                                    supper.
The house does not have to have silver and gold on the
                                                    staircase;
No more does music need elaborate instruments;
Indeed life can be quite pleasant stretched out on the grass
Beside a river, in the shade of a suitable tree.
That is a pleasure involving no great expenditure,
Particularly delightful when the weather is hot
And in neglected fields which have a few flowers.
If you find yourself in bed with a raging temperature
Recovery does not depend on expensive furniture
And some people have got better on a straw mattress.

Since ingots of gold can do no good to our bodies,
Nor indeed can a pedigree or political power,
One must conclude they do not serve our minds either
Except perhaps in so far as the sight of your army
Performing manoeuvres specially for you to review,
Or the spectacle of your fleet putting out in the channel
Gives you a moment's distraction from your religion
And your anxieties at the approach of death
Leaving your mind to benefit by its emptiness.

But if you see that such a hope is ridiculous
And that in fact men's fears and anxieties
Are not erased by expensive martial noises,
So that even outrageously powerful political figures
Feel them in spite of all the flashing equipment
And even the best padded uniforms cannot deaden them,
How can we doubt that only reflection can quieten us
In a life which, after all, is passed in shadows?

For just as children are afraid of the dark,
Their elders as often as not are afraid in the light
Of things which really there is as little cause to fear
As those with which children contrive to frighten themselves
These grown-up terrors are also no more than shadows
And yet they are nothing that sunlight can dissipate:
What is needed is the rational study of nature.

So now I will tell you how the genetic particles
Bring different things into being and then dissolve them,
How they move, and what the forces are which control them,
With what velocity they are propelled through the emptiness:
These are the issues for which I require your attention.

Matter is certainly not glued firmly together,
Since everything we see wears out and grows less
So that everything seems to flow away in the end,
Concealing its final decrepitude from our eyes
While the universe as a whole somehow goes on.
This is because the particles which escape
From one object attach themselves to another
And so one thing will grow old and another flower.
That is not all: for everything is renewed
And mortals live by preying on one another.
Some kinds of creature increase, while others diminish;
In a little time there is a new generation,
As the torch is handed on by Olympic runners.

There are those who think that particles can stop moving
And then start again after reaching a point of rest,
But that is an intellectual deviation.
For, since it is through emptiness they move,
Each must be carried along by its own weight
Or else by impact from another particle:
For if they hit one another they jump away:
Hardly surprising, since they are very hard bodies,
Heavy and solid, with nothing at all behind them.

To understand how matter is agitated
You have to remember the universe has no bottom
Nor any other point at which things can stop,
And since space is without limit and cannot be measured
It spreads out on every side in more than immensity,
— A point which has already been fully demonstrated.

With this arrangement, no question of any particle
Being anywhere at rest in the emptiness,
But all are moved for ever with varying movements.
Some hit and rebound to a considerable distance,
While others recoil but a little way from the shock;

And the ones which are separated by smaller intervals
Are those whose shapes are such that they get entangled:
These form the substance of the hardest rocks and of iron
And other things of similar weight and density.
Those particles which jump a long way apart
— And these are, relatively, a small number only —
Leaving wide spaces between, make up such substances
As the thin air and the bright rays of the sun.

Many particles wander in the great emptiness,
Some of them strays and rejects from substances,
Some have found no group that they could belong to.
A model and image of such wandering particles
Is something we have daily before our eyes:
Just look when sunbeams shine in a darkened room;
You will see many tiny objects twisting and turning
And moving here and there where the sunlight shows.
It is as though there were an unending conflict
With squadrons coming and going in ceaseless battle,
Now forming groups, now scattering, and nothing lasting.
From this you can imagine the agitation
Of the genetic particles in the great emptiness,
So far at any rate as so small an example
Can give any hint of infinite events.

Or you might say that it is worth while to study
The way in which the motes of dust dance in a sunbeam
Because the behaviour of these tiny objects
Gives us a notion of that of invisible particles.
You will see many of these sailing dust-motes
Impelled no doubt by collisions one cannot detect,
Change direction, and turn off this way or that.
Surely their movement depends on that of the particles.

The particles are of course the first things to move;
Then it is the turn of the smallest groups
Which are, so to say, the next in the order of forces
And are shaken by an impulse from the particles
Till they in turn hit something a little bigger.
So movement arises from the original particles
And continues in series until it reaches our senses
And we see at last the motes which dance in the sunbeams,
Though even at this stage collisions are not perceptible.

Memmius, my next subject is the velocity of particles
And it can be disposed of in very few words.
When first the dawn comes scattering its new light
And the miscellaneous birds, here and there in the woods,
Begin to fill the air with their fluid song,
How suddenly does the sun as it rises up
Pour its light over everything! This is a spectacle
Which we have witnessed over and over again.
And yet the warmth that the sun puts out, and the light,
Do not travel in absolute emptiness, there is something to
                                        hinder them;
They have to swim, so to speak, through waves of air.
Moreover, the particles of heat do not come singly
But tangled up or joined together in masses;
So they impede one another, and find themselves bumping
Against other particles; their travel is relatively slow.
But the original particles, heavy and dense,
Travelling through the great emptiness — nothing impedes
                                        them
No doubt because they are so much of a unity —
Are carried forward without any change of direction.
They must certainly be distinguished for speed
And move much faster than the rays of the sun,
Passing over the same distance in much less time
Than it takes sunbeams as they move through the sky.

   .   .   .   .

Nor to follow each of the particles separately
To see how it is that each one is carried on.

There are those who, ignoring the nature of matter,
Consider that nature without some divine assistance
Could not so aptly provide for human requirements,
Changing the annual seasons, making crops ripen;
And all the other things which persuade human beings
To follow their pleasure and, under the guidance of Venus,
Ensure that the human race does not die out.
And those who imagine this all a divine invention
Designed to benefit man, are wide of the truth,
For if I did not know what I do about elements
I should still be prepared to assert, from the look of the sky
And the observation of many other phenomena
That it is absurd to talk of a nature created

For human use, I could think of so many improvements:
As I will explain to you, Memmius, a little later.
But now I had better get on with explaining motion.

This is, I think, the place for my demonstration
— Which you should attend to — that no sort of physical
object
Can of itself be carried or travel upwards.
The way in which flames behave should not deceive you.
They are created upwards and so they grow;
But so do ripening crops and trees grow up
Although the weight that is in them pulls them down.
Nor is it to be supposed that when flames leap up
To the roofs of houses and eat up the rafters and beams
They act of their own volition with nothing to force them.
The same phenomenon may be observed when blood
Spurts from the body and fountains high in the air.
And haven't you seen how timber dropped into water
Is as it were spat to the surface? If we press it down,
The harder we press, the greater the force we exert on it,
The keener the water becomes to vomit it back
And more than half of it jumps up above the surface.
Yet nobody doubts that any material of this sort,
Which found itself in the void, would be carried down.
The principle is the same for the action of flames
Which must be pressed upwards although their weight
carries them down.
And haven't you seen the night sky streaked with the flames
Of heavenly bodies which carry the marks as they ride
In whatever direction nature opens a way for them?
Have you not seen stars falling and reaching the earth?
The sun itself drops warming rays to the ground
From the summit of heaven and sows the fields with its light
So that must be the direction its heat would take
Just as you may see lightning break through a rain-storm
With flashes from every side as it runs through the clouds
And falls to the ground as the force of the flame directs it.

There is something more to be learned about this matter:
When bodies are borne on down and down through
emptiness
By their own weight, at a moment one cannot fix

At uncertain points in space, they give way a little
To one side or another in a slight deflection.

If they did not, then everything would fall down,
Like drops of rain falling for ever through emptiness,
There would be no occasion for encounters of elements
And if one did not strike another there would be no creation.

For if anyone thinks that the heavier bodies could
Fall on the lighter, because they fall down more swiftly,
And that this could be the origin of the encounters
Which bring about the movements of generation,
They are certainly wandering a long way from the truth.
Anything falling through water or through the air
No doubt must gain in speed as it has more weight
Because the body of water and the nature of air
Are such that they cannot offer equal resistance
To everything, but give way fast to the heaviest:
But emptiness has no power of resisting anything
At any time whatsoever or any place;
Its nature is to give way, and so it does.
It follows that the void is passive and everything falls
Through at equal speed whatever its weight
And therefore there is no question of lighter elements
Being fallen upon from above, so having encounters
Which might produce the movements required by nature.

It is clear as day there must be some slight deflection
In elements as they fall, but only the slightest;
We must avoid the suggestion of slantwise motion
For it is a matter of common observation
That heavy bodies do not fall out of the vertical.
If they fall they fall, you have only to look to see this.
Yet to say that nothing suffers the slightest deflection
Is to go beyond what observation shows.

And then, if every movement follows another
In perfect sequence, and everything is determined,
The elements never suffering that slight deflection
Which could start something and break the order of fate
So that cause does not follow cause for the whole of
                                                    infinity,

How would living creatures everywhere come by that
                                              freedom
Which enables the will to wrench itself loose from fate
And us to go up and down the world as we like?
We change direction not because it is time to do so
Or because we are where we must, but because we want to.
Without a doubt, in these things our several wills
Are what starts the movement which is then carried out
                                    through our limbs.
Haven't you seen, at the moment the barriers open
At the start of a race, the horses as if hesitating,
Unable to throw themselves forward as fast as they want to?
The whole of their matter has to be brought into motion,
Which means that the messages have to run through their
                                              bodies
Till every bit is alerted and moves with the mind.
As you see, the impetus comes from within in the first place;
The movement starts in the mind and in the will;
From there it spreads through the limbs and through the
                                    whole body.

It is not at all the same thing when we move at the the
                                              instance
Of *force majeure*, or simply because someone pushes us.
In that case the material of the whole body
Obviously moves in spite of us, hurried onwards
Until the will succeeds in pulling it up.
The fact is that external forces may move us
And hurry us onwards by the scruff of our necks
Yet in spite of this there still is something inside us
Which can put up a struggle and get in the way of them.
It is this which controls the material of our bodies
And by a certain adjustment of our limbs
Brings them up in their flight and returns them to rest.

There must for this reason be in the elements
Some cause of movement other than weights and collisions
From which we could derive our innate free will:
For we know nothing is ever produced from nothing.
The existence of weight means that all is not done by
                                              collision,
As it were by external force; but the mind would be down

To inner necessities for our very least action
And so defeated as to suffer and bear without choice
If it were not for the tiny deflections which happen to
                                                    elements
In times and places which are in no way determined.

The total supply of matter was never more close-packed
Than it is now, nor was it ever more scattered:
For nothing is added to it or taken away.
And so the movement of elements at the present
Is exactly as it has been in times gone by,
Which is just the same as it will be in the future:
The way that things have been produced is the way that
                                                    they will be,
The same conditions of being and growth and strength
As each thing has been given by the law of nature
Will continue, and nothing will change the whole of nature.
For there is nothing outside it to which any matter
Could make an escape; nor again is there anything anywhere
From which a new force could break in and so change
The course of nature, or disrupt the pattern of movement.

It is nothing to wonder at, when you think about it,
That although the elements are in ceaseless motion
The universe as a whole appears to be stationary
Except so far as particular bodies are moving.
We are dealing with things which are too small for perception
When we speak of elements: and since the bodies themselves
Are too small to be seen, so naturally are their movements.
Indeed, with things which are visible, there is concealment,
Often, of movements, which distance can often erase.
For example, when flocks of sheep are devouring a hillside,
Drifting about as the sparkling dew on the pasture
Tempts them to this bit or that, while the lambs full of milk
Play round the ewes, or amiably butt one another:
All this is completely confused from a distance
And looks like a patch of white on the green of the hill.
In the same way it happens that legions may be on exercise,
Filling the plain with an imitation battle,
With cavalry dashing about and making the ground shake;
The flashes of their arms and their armour reaching the sky
And making the earth seem brilliant as well as noisy;

The whole accompanied by vociferous shouting
Which echoes from mountains and seems to go up to the
                                                                        stars
Yet there will be a place high up in the mountains
From which all this looks like a bright spot on the plain.

Now let us look at the nature of the elements
And how they differ from one another in shape;
You will see that there is extraordinary variety:
Not that the number in any one group is small
But that in general they are not completely alike.
No wonder: since the stock of them is so great,
Unlimited, as I have said — one might say, infinite —
There is plenty of room for variety and it would be odd
If all of them were of identical size and shape.

And then take a look at mankind, or at shoals of fish
Swimming about, or herds of cattle, wild beasts
Or the different sorts of bird which haunt the water,
Swooping by river banks or springs or pools;
And those which prefer the quiet of deep woods:
If you examine a group of one species
You will find that there are differences between them.
How else indeed could the young bird know its mother,
Or the mother bird its young; as we see they do,
For they recognize one another as well as we do.

So, when a young beast falls in a cloud of incense
Before the elaborate shrine of some god or other
And as it dies squirts a river of blood:
Its mother, as she wanders over the meadows,
Knows which footprints her own calf has left
And casts her look in every direction, hoping
To find it again at last: and fills with her lowing
The woods and hills around her, and often goes back
To her shed hurt through and through by desire for her calf.
Neither new-sprung willows, nor grass growing strong on
                                                                        the dew,
Nor rivers flowing smoothly and full to the brim
Can give her pleasure or turn her mind from mourning;
No more can sight of other calves at their grass
Distract her mind or alleviate her care:
Her search is specific and she knows what she's looking for.

Just so do kids, when they raise their quivering voices,
Seek their particular nannies, and new lambs
Know the bleat of their mothers: for nature demands
That each of them find its way to particular udders.

Or take any ear of corn: you will never find one
Whatever kind you go for, in which there are not
Detectable differences between the grains.
The same variety can be seen in shells
Of various colours which decorate the sands
Licked by the water in the lap of the bay.
Everything goes to show that on the same principles
— They are natural products and not artificially made —
The elements do not follow a single pattern
But flutter around in space with different shapes.

It is easy enough to explain why a streak of lightning
Has so much more penetration than a flame
Of the sort which flickers off the top of our torches.
You may say that the fire from the sky is much more subtle
And that the elements it consists of are smaller
So that it easily finds its way through interstices
Impermeable by the flame of a torch made of pine.

In the same way light can travel through sheets of horn
But rain cannot: why, if it were not that the elements
Which make up light are smaller than those of water?

And wine will run through a strainer as fast as you like
While oil will dawdle and go through drop by drop;
Either the elements making up oil are bigger
Or else they are hooked and catch on one another,
Which means that they cannot very easily separate
As they have to do in order to go through the mesh
Because they must go through the openings one by one.

Or take the case of liquids like honey and milk
Which leave a pleasant sensation upon the tongue
In contrast with the bitter flavour of wormwood
Or centaury, whose flavour puckers the mouth:
You can easily see that smooth and rounded elements
Must form the things agreeable to the taste

While things which are bitter and rough upon the palate
Are composed of hooked and implicated elements
And because of that have to cut their way through our senses
Breaking open the organs to find a way in.

Things which are disagreeable to the senses,
And things agreeable, are made up of different shapes:
You should not imagine that, say, the screech of a saw
Is made of elements of the same smooth texture
As those which make up the most musical sounds
Which can be evoked by strings plucked by skilled fingers.
Nor do you have the same shapes in your nostrils
When you smell, for example, putrid corpses burning
And when you are in a place just strewn with saffron
Or near an altar censed with Arabian perfumes.

And do not attribute a similar composition
To the sort of colours on which the eye can feed
And those which prick the eyeballs and force your tears,
Or else so disgusting you have to turn away.

For every sort of sight which pleases the senses
Has been created out of some smooth elements
While on the other hand things which look unpleasant
Will always contain some elements which are rough.

There are also elements neither entirely smooth
Nor yet, so to speak, entirely covered with prickles
But rather with some slight protuberances
Which tickle the senses rather than actually hurt them:
In that class you may put tartar and elecampane.

You will note also that blazing fires and cold frost
Bite the senses in quite dissimilar ways
As a touch of either of them will quickly prove.
Touch, ah, touch, you may well invoke the gods for it,
It *is* the sense of the body, and whether for outer things
Or for the stresses in the body itself.
It may be either the various genital pleasures
Or else a blow which shakes up the whole of the body,
You find the elements thrown into confusion.
You may try a small experiment for yourself

By touching yourself with your hand on any part.
Isn't it obvious the elements must differ widely
In shape, to produce such contrasting effects on the senses?

And then, the things which seem to us hard and close-packed
Must be largely composed of hook-like elements
Which intertwine and so hold themselves together.
In this class first of all you may put the diamond
Which will stand up to anything in the way of blows
And flints and iron, for example, which have some strength
And brass which screams as it clings to the turning hinge.

Some things must be made of smooth round elements
— Such obviously must be the case with liquids
For the several drops show no signs of holding together
And roll away downwards as soon as they get the chance.

As to the sort of things that dissipate easily
— Such as smoke, for example, or mists, or flames — it
                                        must be
That even if they are not entirely made of round and smooth,
They are made of elements which do not catch on each
                                        other
Or are so formed as to prick us, or travel through rocks:
They do not stick together, it is easy to see
And that simple fact is quite enough to show
That they are not made of tangled elements but as it were
                                        needles.

It is true there are liquids which also seem to sting us,
As sea-water does, but that should cause no surprise;
Where there is fluid there are certainly smooth round
                                        elements
But smoothness and roundness can be mixed with
                                pain-giving qualities.
One hasn't necessarily to think of hook-like elements,
A certain roundness is quite consistent with roughness;
You could have a shape which would roll, but still cause
                                        discomfort.

This mixture of rough and smooth in sea-water
Becomes more credible if you consider the method

56

Of separating the two and seeing them apart.
The salt water sweetens itself when you pass it through
                                                    filters
And it flows through layers of earth till it comes out fresh.
It leaves the rougher elements up on the surface
To which their roughness enables them to cling.

Here I would add a refinement to my theory
Which follows from what I have said: that the elements
Have only a finite variety of shapes.
If it were otherwise, some elements necessarily
Would have themselves to be of infinite size.
As long as they are small there is no possibility
Of more than a limited variation in shape.
Imagine an element divided in three small parts,
Or not much more; then try to arrange those parts
In any manner you will, in a single body.
You can put the top to the bottom or the left to the right
And try any other combination of changes
To produce a modification of the whole shape:
You will soon arrive at the point where, to effect any change,
You will have to add new parts; and if you continue
With new arrangements, you will find for similar reasons
That you will never have done with adding new parts.

You will see that increase of size will follow inevitably
From multiplication of shapes: and you cannot believe
In an infinite variety in the shape of elements
Without admitting that some are of monstrous proportion;
I have shown that this is something you cannot prove.

Why, the brilliant cloths we get from the barbarians,
Meliboean purple, dye from the shells of Thessaly,
The very peacocks with their astonishing beauty
Would soon be superseded by other colours;
No one would think anything more of myrrh or honey;
The song of the swans and the sweet sound of stringed
                                                    instruments
Would be surpassed and so reduced to silence
For there would always be something better than they.
Or everything could just as well deteriorate
And you would get the same process in reverse:

57

Things would become increasingly offensive
To our noses and ears and eyes and to our taste.
But since none of these things happens and there are limits
To what you may experience in either direction
It follows that matter has a fixed number of shapes.

Likewise, from fire to the freezing frosts of winter
Is a finite distance, whichever way you look at it;
Between them is every degree of heat and cold
And altogether these make up a perfect series.
So created objects differ in finite ways
Since the bounds of their sensible qualities are so marked
At one end by flames, at the other end by hard frost.

To this I would add another not unconnected point;
It is that the number of elemental bodies
Which are of similar shape, is bound to be infinite
For, since the number of shapes has been shown to be finite,
It must be, for otherwise you would be asserting
That the supply of matter is limited; which it is not,
As indeed I showed, in a few not ill-sounding verses,
When I was explaining how material elements
Out of the infinite hold up the ordered universe
By raining upon it a continuous series of blows.

You see certain animals are rarer than others
And observe perhaps that they are by nature less fertile,
But there may be in other regions, in far-off lands,
Many of them to keep the numbers up:
That is the case among the quadrupeds,
With the elephant which has a hand like a serpent:
In India there are thousands, a wall of ivory
Making the country impenetrable: such are the numbers
There, of an animal which we think of as rare.

Yet I will concede if you like that there may be creatures
Produced which are the only ones of their kind
And have not got their like anywhere in the world;
But if the supply of matter were not infinite
They could not possibly be conceived or born,
Moreover could not feed themselves or grow.

For suppose the elements of one of these unique bodies,
Scattered indifferently round the universe,
Whence, where, how would they meet to be productive
In the great sea of matter and alien elements?
They would have no reason, I think, to come together.
It is rather as, after a series of terrible shipwrecks
The sea throws up its debris along the coast,
Spars, rudders, masts and every sort of equipment
As if by way of warning to human beings
That they should always think of the sea as an ambush
And keep away, and never trust to it
When it smiles and shows itself at its most calm.
Just so, if you limit the number of certain elements,
They must for all time be scattered and swept up and down
And carried as it were here and there by the tides
And never come together in combination
Or stay in a group which could grow into something
                                        noticeable;
Yet this is something which happens every day
For things are created and once created they grow;
It is evident therefore that every kind of element
Exists in infinite number and all needs are supplied.

So the movement to death cannot have it all its own way
Nor can it finally bury all life from the light,
But no more can the movement of life and growth
Keep things going for ever in its direction.
There is as it were a battle among the elements,
Never lost or won and stretching away through all time.
For a time the vital elements have it their way
And then they are overcome; so mourning is mixed with
                                        the wail
Of the newborn infant saluting the shores of light.
No night ever followed a day, and no dawn a night
Without someone hearing the tiny cry of an infant
Mixed with the chorus of tears you get at a funeral.

There is one point you should always keep in mind
And never let it escape your memory:
This is that nothing ever appears in nature
Which is composed out of a single element
Or which is not made up of a mixture of several

And that a greater variety of qualities
And potential in anything will indicate
That it combines elements of various shapes.

Earth in the first place has in it all the elements
From which the springs renew the seas with their freshness;
She also has the matter needed for fire
And at many points there is burning under the ground
And this is the source of Etna's eructations.
The shining harvests and the delightful fruit-trees
We find so useful, she has means to produce all of them,
To say nothing of streams and foliage and pasture
For all the wild animals wandering around in the hills.

That is why she is called the Great Mother and mother of
                                                    beasts;
She is the actual progenitor of our bodies.
The wise old poets of Greece have represented her
Sitting back in a chariot and driving two lions
High in mid-air, by way of making the point
That the earth must not be thought of as resting on earth.
They chose wild beasts as an indication that offspring,
However wild, are bound to submit to their parents. ·
They put a crown like a wall around her head
Because there are towns and fortresses in high places.
It is with these insignia that the Great Mother
Is carried about now amidst a general shudder.

It is she whom nations still in the old tradition
Call the Mother of Ida. They give her Phrygian servants
To accompany her, because it was from Phrygia,
They say, the first corn came, now grown the world over.
They give her gelded priests, because those who violate
The maternal mystery and turn against their parents,
Can only, according to them, be judged unworthy
Of bringing any progeny to the light.
They beat taut drums with their hands and there are
                                                    cymbals,
Hollow, and there is the raucous sound of the trumpet
And the Phrygian flutes to pitch the mind up higher.
They carry weapons to signify the fury
Directed against the thankless and impious mob
And to fill them with a proper fear of the goddess.

And so, as soon as she is drawn through the city,
Bringing a blessing to mortals by her presence,
The inhabitants throw copper and silver coins;
A large donation is best: and a storm of roses
Falls on the Mother and does not miss her attendants.

A band of armed men the Greeks call Phrygian Curetes
Amuse themselves by playing about with weapons,
Jumping up and down rhythmically, glad to spill blood,
Shaking the terrifying crests on their heads;
They are like the Dictaean Curetes who once
Covered the wanderings of Jupiter in Crete
While all around children in agile chorus,
Carrying arms, strike bronze on bronze in time,
So that Saturn shall not discover and eat his son
And so cause irremediable grief to the mother.
It is for this the Great Mother has her warriors
Or else to signify the value of arms
And courage in defence of one's native country
And to say that those who have parents should protect them.

All this is very well or at least seductive
But I am afraid it is very far from the truth.
The nature of the gods is such that they cannot
Do otherwise than enjoy their peace for ever
Without the slightest concern for our affairs.
They have no experience of discomfort or danger;
They have their resources and they want nothing from us;
They are not impressed by our merits or touched by our
                                                    anger.

The earth indeed is always quite insensible
But as the repository of many elements
She brings a vast array of things to the light.
If anyone likes to say 'Neptune' instead of 'the sea'
Or 'Ceres' instead of 'corn', or indeed say 'Bacchus'
Instead of giving the proper name to the liquid,
We might as well let him, and let him declare that the earth
Is the mother of gods — provided, of course, he can keep
His mind quite free of any taint of religion.

Often you find sheep, horses and herds of cattle
Feeding together off the selfsame grass

And they always move under the selfsame sky
And satisfy their thirst by drinking from rivers;
They live in their different kinds and they keep the nature
Each of them has from his parents, and follow their ways:
So much diversity is there in the matter
Contained in the grass, and so much in the rivers.

Or take an animal — any one you like —
Consider its bones, blood, veins, heat, moisture and sinews;
It gives you some idea of what different elements
Of different shapes, are needed to make such organs.

Then anything that can be burnt must contain at least
The elements necessary for forms of fire;
Which means what will set things on fire, what will send
                                              out light,
What will send out sparks and scatter embers about.
Go over in your mind the whole range of nature,
You will find that everything has a number of elements
And somehow holds together quite different shapes.

There are many things which have both colour and taste
As well as smell; this is true of many offerings.
These clearly must consist of various elements
For smell goes into the limbs and colour does not
While colour and taste have their own way to the senses
Which must suggest elements of different shapes
And seem to prove that unlike forms will combine
So that things indeed are made up of a mixture of elements.

And so of course it is in these very verses,
For many letters are common to many words
And yet you have to admit both the words and the verses
Differ clearly enough and are made of different elements:
No two are of identical composition
But as a rule they do not all resemble each other.
And so in other things there are common elements
But that does not mean that, looked at as a whole,
They do not differ widely from one another.
You might as well say there could not be common elements
In corn and fruit and in the human race.

But do not imagine that anything can be joined
To anything: that would give us a world of monsters,
Creatures half men, half beasts, and in the branches
Of trees one would see living creatures born:
Many a cow would appear with a fish's tail
And every land which has its crop of quadrupeds
Would produce some nightmare animals breathing flame.
Since we see nothing of that we may assume
Each sort of body comes from a special seed
And as it grows it remains true to its kind.

All this indicates, surely, a certain order.
For everything takes what it needs from the food it eats
And that goes into its limbs and gives them their movement:
On the other hand the matter which is not needed
Nature throws out on the ground: and besides invisible
Matter is always being thrown off from every body
Just as matter rains from outside: and the bits that go
Are those not apt for that particular whole.

Do not imagine that it is only animals
Who are subject to such laws: the laws govern everything.
There are things which are quite different
From one another — whole worlds apart — and it must be
That elements of different shapes are at the bottom of it;
Not that there are not many of similar form
But still a total resemblance is unusual.

And if the elements differ, there must be a difference
Between them in distances, travel, connection and strike
As they come together or move; and not only animals
Are differentiated in this way: but land and sea
Are so divided: and the sky and earth kept apart.

Another point now from my delightful studies.
You should not suppose the whiteness you see in an object
Means whiteness in its elements, or that black objects
Come from elements which themselves are black;
Nor indeed, whatever colour an object has,
That it is made of elements of that colour.
The elements of matter have no colour at all,
Neither like the objects they form nor yet unlike them.

63

If you think that colourless bodies are inconceivable
I can only tell you that you are a long way out.
For those who are born blind and have never seen
The light of the sun, yet still know bodies by touch
From the earliest age, with no conjunction of colour.
So it is evident that the mind can form
An idea of objects without the assistance of colour;
And we ourselves find, touching things in the dark,
That we feel them, though we have no sensation of colour.

May I now reinforce the point by a little theory?
Any colour can change into any other
— Which is not consistent with the nature of elements.
There must be something unchangeable in the elements
If everything is not to turn into nothing,
For nothing can change so as to change its nature
Without the extinction of what it was before.
Do not therefore attribute colour to elements;
You would be on the way to destroying the whole creation.

On the other hand, if you take it there is no colour
In elements, but that they are of various shapes
Which can produce and change the whole range of colours;
And if you go on to attribute a proper importance
To their position and movements and interrelations;
You will find no difficulty in explaining how
Something which a moment before was black as coal
Should suddenly change and look as white as marble:
As the sea, when tremendous winds have stirred up its
                                                   waters,
Is turned into waves which look exactly like marble.
You could say that something we often see as black
Will, when there is some disorder in its elements
And some are added and some taken away
Appear immediately as a shining white.
If the elements of the sea were in fact sea-blue
They could not be white, it is as simple as that:
But however you jumbled them up they would still be blue
And nothing could ever turn them into white.

If it were out of elements of various colours
That the pure and uniform skin of the sea was made

64

In the way that out of miscellaneous shapes
You might construct, for example, a perfect square,
Then you would expect, as in the square you could see
The dissimilar shapes that made it, so in the sea
Or in any other thing with a uniform surface
The various contrasting colours make it up.

Besides, with the various shapes which might make a square,
There is no conflict between the part and the whole:
But variety in the colours which make up a surface
Are a real impediment to its uniformity.

And anyhow, it does not help the theory
Which would attribute various colours to elements
If the argument is, not that white things are made of white
                                        elements
And black of black, but that both are made from a mixture
Because whiteness would certainly be produced more easily
From colourless elements than, let us say, from black
Or indeed from any colour which is contrary to it.

And since without light there cannot be any colours
And elements do not emerge in the light at all
It must be that they are in fact without colour.
What sort of colour can there be in pitch darkness?
Doesn't colour change with the light and in fact depend
On whether the light falls directly or indirectly?
Take a look at a pigeon in the sunlight
And the little feathers about its neck and head;
Sometimes they flash and you might be looking at rubies;
Another time, it may be, the impression you get
Is of something between sky-blue and emerald.
A peacock's tail spread out in a brilliant light
Gives off all colours as it turns in the sun.
It is by the fall of light that colours are made
And one cannot conceive that they could exist without it.

And since what affects the eye is a sort of blow
On the pupil, when it is said to be seeing white,
And so with black and all the other colours;
When you touch something colours are irrelevant,
The thing that matters about it is the shape:

So one may say that elements don't need colours;
Their shapes alone give different tactile impressions.

If the colours of elements don't depend on their shapes
In any rigorous way, but are simply whatever
They turn out to be, without any rhyme or reason,
Why then are the things composed of them not equally
Apt to take on any colour by chance?
You would think you would often see a crow fly by
Flapping great wings of the most striking white
And the swans would be black if that's what their elements
were
Or take any other colour in the same way.

The more a body is divided into small parts
The more it loses its colour, and in the end
You can see the colour is put out like a light;
This happens when anyone makes a fine division
Of purple, or scarlet, the most brilliant colour of all;
Take it thread by thread, the colour disappears;
This shows that bits of matter will lose their colour
Before you take the division as far as elements.

Lastly, since it is admitted that not all objects
Emit a sound or a smell, you accept quite readily
That you shouldn't attribute to them a sound or a smell;
So, since we don't see everything with our eyes
We may conclude that some things are without colour,
As there are some which have neither sound nor smell:
The able mind can just as well apprehend these things
As it can objects deprived of other qualities.

You should not suppose that it is only colour
That the elements are deprived of: they have no warmth,
Nor have they any cold, or violent heat;
Nor do they throw off any suggestion of smell.
So, when we are making essence of marjoram
Or a concoction of myrrh or flower of nard,
Which has so sweet a smell; the first thing we need
Is, so far as it can be had, an oil without scent,
Something quite neutral to the sense of smell
So that it may destroy as little as possible
With its pungency, the smell of what is boiled with it.

For the same sort of reason it is necessary that the elements
Should contribute nothing in the way of smell or sound
To objects: they cannot indeed, for they give off nothing.
For the same reason too they cannot bring any taste
Or heat or cold or intermediate temperature,
Or other qualities which are the marks of mortality:
Softness, pliancy, brittleness, crumbling, porousness;
All such qualities must be alien to elements
If there is to be anything of a permanent basis
Which could assure the life of natural objects;
If not, the whole creation would sink to nothing.

Consider now the case of sentient things;
That they are put together from the non-sentient
Is obvious enough: there is nothing in common experience
Which contradicts or conflicts in any way with that:
It is rather as if we were taken by the hand
And forced to believe live creatures come from dead matter.

You can see, for example, living worms come out
Of stinking dung, when the earth itself is putrid
And sodden in consequence of heavy rains.
Everything else is changed in the same way.
Rivers and every kind of herbage turn
Into cattle; the cattle themselves turn into our bodies;
And it is not unusual for our bodies to end
Giving energy to wild beasts, or feeding vultures.

So nature turns all food into living bodies;
The senses of living creatures are made that way;
It is not much different from the way that flames
Are produced from dry wood and all is turned to fire.
Now do you see why it is of some importance
What order the elements move in, how they are blended
And what collisions are apt to take place among them?

Indeed, what is it that strikes your mind, and moves it,
And forces you to express your various opinions,
And to think that the sensible cannot come out of the
                                             insensible?

I am not asserting that stones and wood and earth
Mixed up together will give you a sentient creature.

In all this business you must remember this:
It is not a question of everything which produces
Objects of any kind, producing senses.
You have to consider first how small are the elements
Which make up sensible things, as well as their shapes,
Their movements, their order, their position and so on:
Now lumps of wood and clods of earth are different.
Yet when these things are putrified by rain
They turn up worms; the elements of the material
Have been shaken out of their order by an intrusion;
They group themselves afresh and so produce animals.

If sensible things were made of sensible elements
That would imply that the elements were soft:
Because it is evident that all sensibility
Is connected with viscera, nerves and veins, all of which
We see are parts of perishable bodies.

Yet even supposing the elements everlasting,
You would have to say they have partial sensibility
Or else that each was, so to say, a complete animal.
But parts cannot have sensibility on their own;
Sense looks beyond the member where it operates
And if a hand is severed, or any other part,
It cannot maintain sensation by itself.
All that is left to say is that the elements
Are living creatures, responding to things as we do:
But then how could it be said that they are able
To escape the ways of death if they are animals?
To be a living creature is to be mortal.

But suppose they did not die; when they came together
What would they be but a crowd of living creatures?
We know that men and cattle and wild beasts
When they come together as they do for copulation
Engender nothing but men, cattle and wild beasts.

But if they lose the sense from their own bodies
And take another, why say they had sense in the first place?
You are left in the end without any better solution
Than the one we have proposed: that chickens from eggs

The worms coming out of the ground in rainy weather
Show that sensible creatures can come from insensible
                                                    matter.

It may be alleged that sense can only arise
From insensible things by a special kind of change,
A sort of birth which could bring something new to light;
But it is plain enough there is no such thing as a birth
Unless some elements came together before
And that without some congress there is no change.
In the first place there can be no sense in a body
Until the living thing itself has been generated
Or while the elements to compose it are scattered
In air, rivers, earth, or things that come out of the earth
And have not been able to perform with one another
Those movements by which we all light up our senses
And which give sense to every living thing.

If any living creature is struck by a blow
Harder than it is his nature to bear
He will go under, confused in body and mind.
His elements are all thrown out of place
And so his vital motions are impeded;
Until his matter, shaken in every limb,
Breaks off what ties the body to the soul
And throws her out of doors through every pore.
What can we suppose a heavy blow should do
But shake the elements till they fall apart?

But if it happens the blow is rather less violent
The vital movements left may have their way
And calm the staggering tumult it produced,
So that the elements go back into their courses
And the movement to death which was so nearly dominant
Is shaken so that the senses burn again.
How else explain how, from the threshhold of death,
A creature can collect himself and return
Instead of following the course and disappearing?

Again, when there is pain, the elements
Out of which the viscera and the limbs are constructed
Are touched by a force which moves in the very depths;

And when those elements reassemble in place
There is smoothness and pleasure: so it is clear that the
                                                    elements
Do not themselves know either pleasure or pain,
Because they have themselves no constituent bodies
Which could get out of place and attempt new movements
Or enjoy any pleasure on the resumption of peace.

But if in order to be able to feel
A creature must be made of feeling elements
What would you say of the elements composing us?
Surely they would have to be able to laugh,
And tears would have to go rolling down their cheeks.
They would discuss the composition of bodies,
Inquiring about their own make-up and origin;
And since they would have to resemble complete human
                                                    beings,
They would themselves have to be composed of elements
Which in turn would be composed . . . and where would
                                                    you stop?
There is no escape: if a creature could speak, laugh, think,
He would have to be made of others which did the same.
And yet one can see that that is a lot of rubbish.
A man can laugh although not made of laughing bits,
And think, or even reason like a philosopher,
Without being made of oratorical elements.
Why then not say that a sensible creature may
Be made of a mixture of elements lacking all feeling?

For we are all of us come from ethereal seed,
There is one father for all, from whom the earth
Receives the drops of fertilizing moisture
And so produces shining crops and trees
And the human race: as well as all wild beasts.
For she provides the food on which all feed
And live their happy lives and get their young.
Therefore she may indeed be called a mother.
What comes from earth, goes back again to earth
And what has been sent from the edge of ether
Is carried back and welcomed by the sky:
But do not think the everlasting elements
Are what you see flow on the surface of things
Which are born at one time and as quickly perish.

70

Death does not wipe out elements, what it does
Is to break up the groups and combinations
So as to make fresh ones from the same material;
His work is rather the changing of forms and colours
Or giving sense and taking it back in a moment;
So you can see, I hope, the importance of elements,
How they are sorted and what their position is
And that collisions may take place among them.
For the same characters spell sky, sea, earth,
Rivers and sun: or corn, trees, living creatures
And even in these verses they are the same,
What matters is what goes with them and how they are
                                                    placed;
If all were not alike, still, for the most part
There is a resemblance: the position is what matters.
So with material things, it is the intervals,
Travel, connections, weight and the collisions,
Their coming together, movements, order and shape
And when these change, the things themselves must change.

Now turn your mind towards the truth of reason.
It is new matter now that will reach your ears,
Something to make the sum of things seem different.
Nothing is ever so easy it does not seem difficult
The first time you try to take it in,
Nor anything so great a wonder that in time
It ceases to cause even the least surprise.
Consider the clear blue colour of the sky
And all that it contains, the stars that wander in it,
The moon, the incomparable brightness of the sun:
If all these were presented now to mortals
For the first time and suddenly met their eyes,
Could anyone say there was anything more magnificent
Or could any nation have dared to imagine such things?
I think not; for it would be such a wonder.
Yet as it is people are thoroughly weary of looking at them;
They hardly deign to raise their eyes for the purpose.
Do not, I beg you, be so frightened of novelty
As to reject what is reasonable: sharpen your judgement;
Weigh what I say and, if it strikes you as true,
Give in; if false, prepare to come to grips with it.
The mind seeks to understand, in the limitless spaces,

Extending out beyond the walls of the world,
What may be there for the intelligence to grasp
And so to speak flies through space to see what it is.

First then, in whatever direction you travel from here,
To left or right, upwards or downwards, or any way,
There is no end to the universe. I have said it,
The thing itself shouts it; the nature of space will have it so.
Since that is so, the emptiness spreads out infinitely
And elements in unlimited numbers float
In many ways, driven in endless movement,
Can there then be the slightest possibility
That this one globe of earth and this one sky
Should be all there is, and the rest of matter do nothing?
Especially as the world is made by nature
And all the elements crashed into one another
In innumerable ways without result or purpose
Until at last they were thrown into such conjunctions
As suddenly produced the wonderful world,
The earth, the sea, the sky and all living creatures.
Again and again you are driven to this conclusion:
That there must somewhere have been other conjunctions
Like those which ether here holds in her jealous grasp.

Besides, wherever there is matter to hand
And place for it, and no cause to prevent it,
The matter must indeed turn into things.
For if the number of elemental bodies
Is such that a whole age could not reckon it up
And if the force of nature remains the same
To throw the wandering elements to and fro
In the same way as here, it must be admitted
There are other worlds in other parts of the universe
And other races of men and of wild beasts.

Consider moreover that in the whole of nature
There is not a thing unique and without antecedents
And most must be classified as one of a kind.
Take first of all the animals, you will see it is so.
It is so with the wild beasts roaming in the mountains,
The human race itself, as well as the silent
Shoals of fish and all the flying creatures.

72

On the same principle you must admit that the sky,
The earth, the sun, moon, sea and all the rest of it
Are not unique, but there are countless numbers of them;
For these are things which have a term to their lives
And which are as dependent on the body
As any creature of an abundant species.

If you keep these things in mind, nature will seem
To be on her own, free of presumptuous masters,
Doing everything herself with no help from the gods.
For I ask you, the gods, lost in their tranquil peace,
Passing the time nursing their sacred hearts!
Who can rule everything, who can have all space
Safe in his hand as if he held a rein?
Who can turn all the skies, or bring enough
Ethereal fire to warm up all the earths?
Ready in every time and in every place
To make shadows with clouds and shake with thunder
The quiet skies? Then send lightning, which often
Strikes on the gods' own temples, and in desert places
Falls pointlessly, and often misses the guilty
To take instead the life of innocent people?

When the world was born, and after the sea's first day,
After the earth and sun had been formed together,
New matter came to join them from outside;
New elements were thrown in from the great universe:
So sea and earth could grow, and so appeared
The palace of the sky and the high roofs
Were built far from the earth and then air came.
For wherever it came from the great rain of blows
Sent every element to the appropriate object;
Moisture to moisture and earth added to the earth;
The fire joined up with fire, and ether with ether;
Until creative nature finished the job
And brought each substance to its fullest growth
As happens when what passes into the veins of life
Is no more than flows out and passes away.
Then is the time when everything comes to a stop
And nature reins back any further increase.
For when anything that you see is growing happily
And gradually step by step approaches maturity,

It is taking in more elements than it gives out,
For food is readily taken into its veins
And it is not so laxly made that it loses particles
So fast that its age is able to replace them.
Of course our bodies ordinarily lose quite a lot,
That is evident enough: but they take in more
Until the day when they reach the summit of growth.
From then on little by little age breaks us up
And we flow away to the worse side of things.
The larger anything is, the bigger the surface,
Once growth has stopped, the more it scatters around
And elements leave it then in all directions.
Food is no longer easily absorbed in the veins;
Not enough is kept to replace the outflowing tide,
So never all that is needed to make up the loss
As must be done if there is to be renewal.
All bodies perish when the outflow leaves them rarefied;
They succumb at last to the elements from outside.
Food, sooner or later, is not enough for old age,
The body cannot withstand all the shocks from without
Which beat upon it and finally get the better of it.

And so it will be at last with the walls of the world
Which are falling into decay in a crumbling ruin.
(All bodies have need of food for renovation
To keep them upright or merely to sustain them;
But the time comes when the veins cannot take in enough
Or it may be that nature does not provide enough food.)
Already the age is broken, the earth is effete
And can hardly produce small creatures, although it once
Produced all species, including huge wild beasts.
I do not think that the human race came down
On a golden chain from heaven to our low fields;
Nor that the sea invented rocks by lashing them:
But earth produced all these as now she feeds them.
And besides, shining harvests, happy vineyards,
Of her own motion she produced them all;
She gave delicious fruit and happy pastures.
Yet things now barely grow for all her effort;
We tire the oxen and wear the labourer out;
Ploughshares grow thin with scraping the mean fields
Which seem more niggardly the more we work them.

Already the old ploughman shakes his head
To see that all his work has come to nothing:
When he compares the present with the past
He may well praise the fortunes of his father.
He will go on about old times, recalling
How men lived easily on far less land
And plots of ground were smaller . . .
He does not understand that things grow worse,
That all things move to death, worn out by age.

BOOK III

The poet praises Epicurus for his unparalleled contribution to human enlightenment. He denounces the fear of death, which is no more rational than the terrors of children in the dark. Then he examines in detail the nature of the mind and the soul, the animus *and the* anima, *and explains their structure and their relationship with one another and with the body. He then gives proofs of the mortality of the soul, which are implicit in his description of it, and concludes with a further diatribe against the fear of death and myths of punishment after death.*

Out of the terrible shadows, it was you who first raised
a light
To show what is the proper measure of life;
I follow you, nothing better has come out of Greece,
And now where the print of your foot fell I place my own,
Not in jealous competition but out of love
Which constrains me to imitate you. For does the swallow
Set herself against swans? Or the wobbling kid
Think that she should go as fast as a racehorse?
You discovered nature, father: you gave us instruction
And left the whole matter set out in your writings
Where, just as bees help themselves in the meadows,
We can replenish ourselves with your golden sayings;
Golden, I mean they are of permanent value.

As soon as your theory, the product of an intellect
Something more than human, began to make some noise,
The fears that haunt minds disappeared, the walls of the
world
Gave way, and I saw through all space how everything
happens;
The pleasant retreats of the gods themselves could be seen,
Untroubled by winds and with no clouds bringing rain
To splash them, nor snow which the bitter frost has hardened
To make them skip: but always a cloudless ether
Covers and smiles on them in a large light.
But I saw nothing at all of what we call Acheron
Though the earth didn't get in the way and prevent me
from seeing

76

All that was happening in the space under my feet.
These things brought me a certain ethereal pleasure
And yet an awe that nature so by your insight
Should be laid bare and every cover withdrawn.

Since I have made it clear what the principles
Of everything are: elements of various shapes
Floating in space and endlessly in collision,
By which means every kind of thing that there is can be
                                                    made:
It now seems the moment to go on to the mind
And the soul and make their nature clear in these verses,
As well as to throw out headlong the idea of Acheron
Which has disturbed human life to its depths for too long
Spreading the blackness of death over everything
And leaving no pleasure as it should be, limpid and clear.

Men often say that sickness and life in disgrace
Are more to be feared than the Tartarus of death
And that they know that life is no more than blood
Or it may be wind. If they carry things so far,
Do they really need to listen to a theory?
Reflect on the way they behave, you will see what they say
Does not in any way represent what they think.
These are the men who in exile and out of sight
Of their kind, overwhelmed by the filthiest accusations,
Suffering from every calamity you can think of
Live on none the less: and wherever they have got to
They sacrifice black sheep and pour libations
To the gods below: indeed, in time of adversity
They turn more credulously towards religion.
You need to look at a man in doubts and dangers
It is in adversity that you see what he's like;
That is what brings his true voice piping up
And tears off the mask and shows what he really is.

Greed, you say, and the blind appetite for honours
Drive men often beyond the bound of the law
And lead them to crime, as accessaries or as executants.
Day and night they demonstrate they can work
And so hope to come out on top; these sores of life
Are in no small measure inflamed by the fear of death

For to live in general contempt or biting poverty
Are seen as far removed from the pleasures of life
And as it were dawdling before death's door:
From which men, under the lash of unreal terrors,
Hope to escape or nor to see at all:
They must grow rich; if that means bloodshed, it does;
The greedy ones must double what they have
— One murder more will fix it, they will be happy
At their brother's funeral, but still fear their relations.

In a similar manner men are often devoured
By envy: they see before them someone with influence,
Whom people look at, who acquires reputation
While they themselves are in the muck and obscurity.
People will die in the hope of getting a statue;
And often go as far as, for fear of death,
To take a dislike to life and to seeing the daylight,
Committing suicide to avoid the sight of it
And forgetting that death is the cause of all their fears,
That it often makes men shameless, breaks up friendships
And destroys all decency in those who give way to it,
For often men have betrayed their country and parents
Because they hoped to keep away from Acheron.

For as children are afraid in the dark of everything
So even in the light we have our fears
Although there is nothing more to be afraid of
Than what, in the dark, makes children fear what is coming.
To dissipate intellectual fears and shadows
Needs, not the rays of the sun nor the light of day,
But rather the rational study of natural appearances.

First I would say that the mind, or the understanding,
In which the directing consciousness is situated
Is no less a part of man than hand or foot
Or the eyes, which are all to be found in the living creature:
Although there is a whole crowd of experts who take the view
That the sense of mind has no particular seat
But is an essential habit of the body,
What the Greeks call harmony, which is said to make us
Live with sense although there is no mind anywhere:
In the same way that good health is said to be

In the body, although it is not a part one can identify,
So they think that sense of mind not a separate part:
And in that they seem to me completely mistaken.

It often happens that some visible part of the body
Is sick, while a part that we cannot see makes us happy
And it sometimes happens exactly the other way round;
A man can be sad although his whole body feels happy:
In the same way as you can have a pain in your toe
Without the slightest suspicion of a headache.

Besides, when the limbs are in a gentle sleep
And the body lies stretched out in a senseless load,
There is something else in us, which at the same time
Flutters a thousand ways, and contains in itself
Movements of joy and the empty cares of the heart.

Now I will show you that the soul is in the limbs
And that it is not by harmony that the body feels.
The proof is, a man can lose a great part of his body
And yet life will somehow carry on in his limbs;
On the other hand,when a little heat has gone out
And a little air has made its way through his mouth,
Life may at once desert the veins and the bones:
The elements do not all have an equal part
In preserving life and holding the frame together
But the most important are those of wind and heat
Which have a special role in keeping life in our limbs.

And since we have discovered the nature of mind
And of the soul, and that they are parts of a man,
Harmony can be given back to the musicians
And not used for something without a name of its own.
Let someone else take the term. Pay attention to me.

Between the mind and the soul there is a close connection
And they are made out of a single substance,
But the head, so to speak, which dominates the whole body
Is what we call the mind or the understanding
And it is situated in or about the heart.
This is what leaps with fear; and in the same neighbourhood
We are soothed by joy: this then is where the mind is.

79

All the rest of the soul is diffused through the body
And moves at the inclination of the mind.
The mind can know for itself and rejoice for itself
When a thing moves neither the body nor the soul,
And as when we feel a pain in the eye or head
It does not follow that the whole body suffers,
In the same way the mind can suffer by itself
Or can feel joy, when the other parts of the soul,
Throughout the limbs, have no sort of special sensation.
It is true that when the mind feels some vehement fear
The whole of the soul throughout all the limbs is in
                                                    sympathy;
Then we may see sweat and pallor all over the body,
The tongue will falter and the voice will choke,
There is mist in the eyes, ringing in the ears, the limbs faint
So that men will often go under from terror of mind.
It is not difficult to conclude from this
That soul and mind are connected; when the mind is struck
The rest of the body is shaken and struck in its turn.

The same line of reasoning suggests that the mind and the
                                                    soul
Are material: for they propel the limbs,
Rouse the body from sleep or change facial expressions
And indeed control the movement of the whole man:
(None of which could happen at all except by touch
And for touch there must be a body): must it not be
                                                    admitted
There is something of body about both the mind and the
                                                    soul?

For the rest, you notice the mind suffers with the body
And shares all the sensations of the body.
If the point of an arrow, without quite killing a man,
Pierces him and damages bones and nerves,
He is likely to faint and fall limply to the ground.
Once there, as it were the tide in his mind rises
And he feels a vague inclination to get up.
So the mind must partake of the nature of the body
Since the impact of a weapon can make it suffer.

What sort of elements is the mind composed of?
If you listen I will explain this to you.

In the first place, the mind must be a very fine substance
Composed of elements which are extremely small.
This you can see quite clearly from the following:
That nothing seems to equal the speed with which
The mind forms an intention and sets it going.
It must therefore be of such stuff that it can be moved
More rapidly than any object visible to us.
Anything so mobile must necessarily be composed
Of elements which are are both very round and small
So that they can be moved by the slightest impulsion.
Thus water flows on the slightest provocation,
Being made of particles which are round and roll easily
Whereas honey is altogther of firmer consistency;
The liquid is so to speak lazy and slow to act,
Its matter is such that it sticks together more easily,
No doubt because of the nature of the particles
— Not so smooth and not so fine or round.
The lightest breeze takes the top off a heap of poppy-seed
And before long there is nothing of it left,
But to move a heap of stones or of ears of corn
Needs something stronger than that. It is that the smallest
And smoothest bodies are those which have most mobility.
On the other hand those which are of greater weight
And of a rougher surface, have more stability.

Now as the mind is of extreme mobility
It follows that it must be composed of elements
Which are small and smooth and round. And that, dear
                                        Memmius,
Is what I call useful knowledge, and you will find it
Helps you to find your way through many problems.

Another point which shows the nature of mind,
How fine its substance, and in how little space
It would be contained if it were concentrated:
When a man is received into the quiet of death
And his natural mind and soul have been withdrawn,
You can see no diminution of the body
Affecting appearance and weight: death leaves it intact
Except for the vital sense and the vital heat.
So the whole soul must be made of the smallest elements
Joined to the veins, the viscera and the nerves;

For otherwise when it is withdrawn from the body
The exterior contours would not remain as they do
Nor should we find that the body lost no weight:
It is the same with wine when its bouquet has gone,
Or with ointment when its scent escapes in the air,
Or when any substance at all has lost its aroma
But does not look any smaller to the eye
And has in fact not lost any of its weight;
Precisely because it is great numbers of small elements
Which make up smell: and give scent to a whole body.
And so again you see that soul and understanding
Are made up of a number of tiny elements
Which, when they go, take nothing from the weight.

Yet it is not to be thought that the soul is simple.
A certain subtle breath leaves a man at death,
Mixed with heat: and heat will draw air with it;
For heat is something not of uniform nature
And since it is also diffuse, it must happen that elements
Of air will find their way among the interstices.
That already gives you a triple nature for air.

Yet these three are not enough to give sensation
Nor can one accept that any of them would produce
The variations which in turn give rise to thought.
There must therefore be some fourth substance as well
Though it is not anything to which a name has yet been given:
Something more mobile and finer than anything else
And made out of the smallest and smoothest elements:
This is what carries impressions through the limbs:
This stirs first, because of its tiny particles,
Then heat and breath both feel the effect of the motion
And so the air and everything is mobilized:
Blood throbs, then all the inner parts are alerted;
And so at last the bones to the very marrow
Feel the sensation of pleasure, or of pain.

Pain cannot get that far, nor an acute
Sickness find its way in, without upsetting everything;
To the point that there is no room for the breath of life
And bits of the soul escape through every pore.
But generally pain so to speak stops at the surface
And when that happens we can keep hold of our lives.

How these four elements are mixed up and how
They are arranged in order to do their work
Is something it is not easy to put into words;
However, I will explain it as best I can.
The mutual relations and movements of the elements
Are such that none of them can be isolated;
They are mutliple properties of a single body.
It is the same sort of thing that you find in living creatures,
They have smell and colour and taste: yet out of these
Somehow a single body is made up.
So heat and air and the invisible power of breath,
Mixed up, create one nature, together with
That mobile force which causes them to move
And so gives sensitive movement to the whole body.
There is nothing in us that lies more deeply concealed
Or more inside us than this fourth substance:
You might describe it as the soul of the soul.
Just as, in all our limbs and throughout the body
There is diffused the force of mind and soul
Since they are composed of bodies which are small and
                                            scattered:
So this anonymous force, made of tiny particles,
Hides itself; it is indeed the soul of the soul
And dominates the whole through which it is infused.
Just so must breath, air, heat, mixed up together,
Work in the limbs, but so that some one element
Predominates and so controls the whole.
The whole in fact does form a single entity;
For it would not do for heat or breath or air
To act on the senses singly and destroy the whole.

There is heat in the mind, which it takes up in anger;
You can see it then in the flashing of the eyes.
There is cold breath too, such as accompanies fear
And sends a shiver of horror through the limbs;
There is too something of that peaceful air
Which brings the tranquil heart and serene face.
There is most of heat in creatures of violent heart
Whose mind is easily inflamed to anger:
In that kind there is first of all the lion
Who breaks his chest with roaring, or who anyhow
Cannot contain the waves of anger within him.

There is more chilly breath in the mind of a deer
And that quickly fans cold air through its inner parts
Which causes a trembling in every limb.
The ox's nature is one with the peaceful air;
The torch of anger is never so lit in him
That he is covered by billowing clouds of smoke;
Nor ever is he shot through with icy fear:
He is somewhere between the stag and the savage lion.

So it is with men: however education
May give them similar polish, yet each retains
Traces of his first nature in his mind.
It is not to be thought that faults can be so eradicated
That one does not run too quickly into anger,
Another not take fright readily, while a third
May take all things more easily than he should.
In many other things there are great differences
Between men in their nature and behaviour:
I cannot now explain the reasons for this,
Nor find names for the shapes of all the elements
From which these many differences arise.
What, however, I think can be asserted
Is that the traces of original nature
Which reason cannot efface, are very few,
So that nothing can stop us living as the gods do.

This nature is contained in the whole body;
It is the body's keeper and sees to its welfare;
There are common roots by which they stick together
And if you pull them apart both are destroyed.
The same with incense, for to extract the odour
Is far from easy without destroying the nature.
So with the nature of mind and soul, to extract them
Is far from easy, without making all dissolve.
The elements are so involved from the very beginning
They find themselves in an indissoluble partnership:
There seems to be no power in mind or body
For either to feel without the help of the other;
It is by their joint motions our senses are lit up
And fanned into flame through all our inner parts.

The body is never generated by itself,
Nor grows so, nor as you see does it last after death.

It is not the case with it as it is with water
That it can lose heat without disintegration
And remain as it was before: it is not like that
With the limbs at all, for once the soul is gone
They are disturbed to the depths and rot away.
From the very start of life the body and soul
Live together and practise their common movements,
Even while they are still in the mother's womb.
There is no separation except in some sort of disaster:
So you see, since their welfare is so much a joint matter
Their nature must also in a manner be joint.

If anyone says the body does not feel
And thinks that the soul, diffused throughout the body,
Carries this sensibility on its own,
He is going against what must be evident truth.
What explanation of the body's impressions
Is there in the facts that I have pointed out?
When the soul has gone, the body is without feeling;
It loses something which did not belong to itself:
But it loses more than that when it finally dies.

To say anyhow that the eyes cannot see anything
But that the soul looks through them as through an open
door
Goes against the evidence of the eyes themselves.
We often find it hard to bear bright lights;
Our eyes themselves experience some discomfort
— Which doesn't happen to doors; if we look through one
It does not show the slightest trace of fatigue.
And after all, if our eyes were simply doors
It ought to be easier for the mind to see
An object once the doors had been removed.

And in this field you should not adopt the opinion
Of Democritus, greatly as I respect him:
He thought that the elements of mind and body
Were arranged alternately throughout the limbs.
But the elements of the soul are very much smaller
Than those of which our bodies are made up;
Moreover they are less numerous, and disseminated
Throughout the limbs: the most you can say is this:

The distance between the elements of the soul
Is as great as the smallest object of which the impact
Can put our sensibility in motion.
Now we do not feel dust settle on our body,
Nor the powder used in toilet preparations,
Nor the evening mist: nor yet the spider's web
Which sometimes nets us as we walk along;
And there are things which, falling on our heads,
Make no impression: the withered coat of an insect,
Bird's feathers, thistledown too light to fall;
We do not feel every creature walking on our skin
And are not sensitive to each particular footprint
Which gnats and suchlike make upon our flesh.
So many of our elements must be affected
Before those making up the soul, and scattered
Throughout the limbs, begin to feel the impact,
Meet, and collide and bounce away again.

It is the mind which holds life in its circle
And dominates it, much more than the soul does.
Without the mind not the smallest bit of the soul
Can stay for a single moment in the limbs;
It follows the understanding out and away
And leaves the limbs to the full chill of death.
But anyone who has a mind is still alive,
Although his trunk is mangled and his limbs cut off.
The soul may disappear from all his limbs,
He can still live and breathe the air that keeps him alive;
Though deprived, not of all, but of a great part of his soul
He can persist in holding on to life.
When an eye is damaged all round but the pupil is left
The faculty of vision remains alive
Provided you do not destroy the whole of the eyeball
Or cut round the pupil, leaving only that,
Which cannot be done without destroying the eyeball.
But if the tiny middle of the eye is eaten into
Although the rest of the eyeball is intact
The light goes out at once and the shadows follow.
The relationship of the soul and the mind is like that.

Now perhaps I should say that the minds of living creatures
And their tenuous souls have both beginning and end;

It is long since my studies led me to that conclusion;
Now I hope to set it forth in a poem worth your reading.
You can treat both substances under a single name
And when I speak of the soul as being mortal
You can take what I say to apply to the mind as well;
The two are so interconnected, and really one substance.

I have shown that the soul consists of very small elements,
Much smaller than those of which water is composed,
Or mist or smoke: it is in fact much more mobile
And it takes a much smaller impulse to get it moving:
An image of smoke or mist would be enough,
The kind of thing that happens when we are asleep
And dream of smoke billowing up from an altar;
No doubt these impressions are thrown off by objects:
Now, since whenever a pitcher is broken to pieces
You see the liquid pour out in every direction,
And since mist and smoke disappear into the air,
You can take it that the soul is spilt and perishes
Faster, and dissolves more quickly into its elements
When once it has escaped from a human body.
If the body, which is a pitcher containing a soul,
Can hold it no longer when it suffers a shock
Or when the loss of blood has made it porous,
How can you believe air could keep a soul together
Since air is much more rarefied than our bodies?

We feel indeed that our minds are born with the body,
Grow with it and grow old as the body grows old;
For children have slight, weak bodies and lack direction
And their thoughts exhibit corresponding qualities.
Then, when they have grown to their full strength, their
                                                    judgement
And their intelligence are greater too.
Later, when the body has been shaken by age
And the limbs have grown weaker and duller, then you will
                                                    see
The wit limp, tongue talk foolery, and thoughts wobble.
Everything fails and all at once there is nothing.
It follows that the stuff of the soul dissolves
And disappears like smoke swept up in the air

For we see it comes with birth and grows with the child
And, as I have shown, it is worn out with old age.

Consider too that just as we see the body
Susceptible to violent disease and pain,
The mind has sharp cares, suffers from grief and fear:
How should it not also have part in death?

So sometimes in a sickness the mind will wander;
It talks unreasonably, becomes delirious;
Sometimes a lethargy will sink a man
In an unending sleep with his head falling limply.
He hears no voices then and knows no faces
Though people stand round calling him back to life
Their cheeks, or their whole faces, covered with tears.
It must be therefore that the soul will dissolve,
It is so easy for infection to penetrate;
For pain and sickness are the makers of death,
The end of so many men has shown us that.

And why when a powerful wine has penetrated
A man and intoxication spreads through his veins
Does there follow this weight in his limbs, and why do his legs
Totter, his speech grow slurred and his mind go under?
His eyes swim and he shouts and becomes quarrelsome;
And why does all this sort of thing come about?
What reason can there be except that wine
When it is inside the body can trouble the soul?
If anything is disturbed and paralysed
Like that, one may take it that, with a little more force,
It would have no chance of longer life and would perish.

And then, a man may have a sudden attack
Before our eyes, as if he were struck by lightning.
He falls, he foams, he moans, his body shivers,
His wits are gone, he stiffens, he twists and pants
Fitfully, and so till he's exhausted.
It is no doubt the violence of his sickness
Right through his body, churning up his soul
To foam as the waves do when the strong winds lash them.
A moan is forced out by the pain in the limbs
And because all the elements of the voice

Are hurried out pell-mell through the gates of the mouth,
The way they usually take and a well-paved road.
The wits are gone, since the force of mind and soul
Are disturbed and wrenched apart from one another,
That is how I see it, as it were by the same poison.
Then, when the cause of illness has withdrawn
And the bitter fluid has flowed back into its hiding-place,
The man gets shakily up, and gradually
Collects his senses and takes up his soul again.
Since even inside the body the mind and soul
Are so shaken up by sickness and torn apart,
How can you believe that without the body's protection,
In the open air and the wind, they could hold their own?

And we see the mind can be cured like a sick body;
We even find it respond to medical treatment,
Which certainly makes it look as if mind is mortal.
For adding some bits, or changing perhaps the arrangement,
Or taking something, however little, away,
Is what you have to do to alter the mind
Or indeed to change the nature of anything else.
But any sort of addition or subtraction
Is out of the question for anything immortal;
For any departure from a thing's proper limits
Implies the death of what was there before.
The mind which sickens shows the marks of mortality
As does the mind which responds to medical treatment:
So truth will always get the better of error
And block its retreat to stop it running away,
Hitting it over the head to produce conviction.

And when we often see a man go bit by bit
And lose the sense of his body a limb at a time;
First in the feet, the toes and nails grow livid,
Then feet and legs will die, and after that
The footsteps of death march over his other parts.
In this way the soul goes piecemeal, and since it does
And cannot escape as a whole, it must be mortal.
But if you insist on thinking that somehow it manages
To retract itself from the limbs and draw together
And that as it takes the feeling from every part
It concentrates them in a single place,

That place ought to show an increased sensibility.
As nowhere in fact does that, we have to take it
The soul falls into bits, is scattered and dies.
Even if I were to allow the false hypothesis
That the soul could somehow concentrate itself
As the body was deprived of light, it would still be necessary
To admit that the soul is mortal. It does not matter
Whether it perishes when dispersed in the air
Or is stupified, concentrated in a lump;
The whole man loses his feeling bit by bit
As less and less life is left in every part.

Since mind is a part of the man, with a fixed location
Exactly as eyes and ears have a fixed location
And all the other senses which govern life;
And as the hand and eye and nose, if separated
From the rest of us, cannot feel or even exist
But in a short time dissolve in putrefaction;
So the mind cannot live without the rest of the body,
Without the man who serves so to speak as a pot for it;
And if you can imagine some closer connection
Than a pot, think of that; it cannot be too close.

Again, the living powers of mind and body
Are strong in conjunction and so enjoy their life.
Without the body the soul is not of a nature
To issue in living movements; nor can the body
Without the soul endure and have use of its senses.
Just as, indeed, an eye torn out by the roots
Cannot see a thing once away from the rest of the body,
So soul and mind can do nothing by themselves;
Of course not, because, when scattered through veins and
                                                    innards,
Through nerves and bones, their elements are held firmly
And are not free to disperse in several directions;
It is when they are shut in that they have movement
Of the kind that gives sensibility; outside in the wind
To which death throws them, they have no such movements
Because they are not held tight in the same way.
The air itself would be a body, and animated,
If a soul could keep itself together in it
And perform the movements it did in nerves and flesh.

So I come to this point again: the body dissolved,
Which covered it, and the living breath given out,
The mind and its faculties will disappear
And the soul as well, one set of causes for all.

Then, since the body is quite unable to bear
The loss of the soul without going rotten and stinking,
What doubt can there be that, from the depths of the body,
Like collecting and rising smoke, the soul goes out?
And that the reason for the putrid ruin
The body falls to, is that far inside there is movement
In its foundations, when the soul trickles out through the
                                                              limbs
Through all the twists and turns that are in the body
And leaves through the pores? There is abundant evidence
That the soul is distributed and goes out through the body
And that it is broken up in the body itself
Before it slips out and swims away in the air.

Sometimes, while still in the confines of life,
But none the less shaken from some cause or other,
The soul appears to want to leave the body
And as in the last hour the face falls away,
The limbs are limp and all the body is bloodless.
This happens when the mind is in a bad way
Or consciousness has gone and there is bustle
As everyone tries to catch the end of the chain.
The understanding and the power of the soul
Are shaken then, and everything seems to loosen;
A little more, they would certainly break up.
What doubt can there be, that once outside the body,
Weak in the open and deprived of its cover,
Not only can the soul not last for eternity
But cannot subsist even for a moment of time?

There never was a dying man felt his soul
Go safe and sound away out of his body,
Feeling it first pushing its way up his gullet.
It fails at first in some specific part
As all the senses do in their proper places.
But if our understanding were immortal
It would not moan and groan at its dissolution

91

But rather find delight in leaving its garment,
Like a snake or an aged stag when it loses its antlers.

And why is it understanding and reflection
Are never produced in the head or the feet or the hands
But always stick in the place where they belong?
There is a place for everything to be born
And a place for it to continue in once it is made.
The organs and the limbs are so set out
That nothing can ever happen the wrong way round,
For such indeed is the order of things that flame
Does not leap out of rivers nor ice from fire.

Besides if the soul is in its nature immortal
And can feel though separated from the body,
It ought to be provided with the five senses:
That is the only way we can represent
To ourselves souls wandering on the shores of Acheron;
And so the painters and writers of earlier centuries
Have represented souls as still having senses.
But away from the body the soul can have no eye,
No nose, no hands, it can have no tongue or ears
And so it can have no feeling and no existence.

And since we feel certain that the whole of our body
Has a sense of life, and that the whole is living,
If suddenly some force should cut it in two
And separate the one half from the other
There is no doubt that the soul would be divided
And cut in two at the same time as the body:
But a thing which splits and divides up into parts
Certainly has no claim to be called immortal.

They say that when chariots with scythes on the wheels
Cut off limbs in their indiscriminate way
A bit cut off can be seen wriggling on the ground
While the consciousness of the man from whom it is cut
Is unaware of the pain, the blow is so swift;
And that his mind is so intent on the battle
That he tries to continue with what is left of his body
And does not notice his left arm, shield and all,
Carried among the horses by wheels and scythes;

92

Another loses his right arm but presses forward;
Another tries to get up when his leg is gone
And the foot is wiggling its toes on the ground near by.
A head cut off from a trunk still warm and living
Looks like life and keeps its eyes wide open
Until it has given up what remains of the soul.

And think of the snake, reared up upon its tail,
Standing with tremulous tongue: if you take a sword
And cut the whole of its length into many pieces
Each one will twist as long as the wound is fresh,
Bespattering the ground with mess from its inside;
The head will make an attempt to bite the tail
To compensate for the burning wound it feels.
Shall we say that there are souls in all these pieces?
If we do, we are in effect asserting that one
Creature has in its body a number of souls.
One is driven to saying that there has been a division
Of a single soul, when the body has divided
And body and soul, both divided, are both mortal.

And then, if the soul is in its nature immortal
And creeps into the body when we are born,
Why have we no memory of an earlier life
And bear no trace of what we did in it?
For if the mind has undergone such change
That all recollection of things past is gone
It seems to me a state not far from death.
So one must say, the soul that was before
Has died, and what we now have is a new one.

If it is after the body is fully formed
At the time of our birth when we cross into the light
That the vivacious mind is introduced,
It should not happen that it appears to grow
As it does grow, in the blood and with the body;
It should be rather like something in a cage
But spreading freely throughout all the body
Which certainly seems contrary to the facts.
For it is closely joined up through the veins, the flesh,
The nerves, the bones: even the teeth are sensistive,
Toothache shows that, or a mouthful of cold water,

Or suddenly biting on a stone in the bread.
So, once again, it does not do to think of souls
As having no beginning or being exempt from death.
For we could not think of them as so completely part of us
If they had found their way in from outside;
Nor, since they are so closely woven into us,
Does it appear that they can go out unharmed,
Loosening themselves uninjured from every nerve
As well as from every bone and all our joints.

Perhaps you think that, coming in from outside,
The soul flows into every part of us?
All the more likely to perish, so fused with the body,
For anything flowing like that would be soluble
And so would die, being everywhere in the body.
As food, when it passes into our various parts,
Is destroyed and transformed into another nature,
So soul and mind, although intact at their entry
Into the body, would be dissolved flowing through it;
Their particles, so to speak, distributed
In every crack, make up the stuff of that mind
Which now controls our body, though born of another
Mind which disappeared when divided up in our limbs.
That is why one must say that the soul has a beginning
And that it is likewise not exempt from death.

Are there or are there not some bits of the soul
Left in the body when it is dead? If there are,
One cannot fairly say that the soul is immortal
Since when it withdraws it leaves a part of itself.
But if it gets away whole so that nothing is left
Of itself in any interstice of the body
How do corpses, when the flesh is rancid,
Manage to breathe out worms? And where do these creatures,
Boneless and bloodless, swarming and heaving, come from?

You may think that souls from somewhere outside insinuate
Themselves into worms, and that each of them finds a body;
But why, after all, should so many thousands of souls
Congregate in a spot which one has just left?
One question must be asked and brought to an issue:
Do the souls hunt out the elements of worms

And each construct a residence for itself
Or do they find their way into ready-made bodies?
But why they should make a body or take so much trouble
Cannot be explained: for as long as they are without bodies
They drift around free from sickness and cold and hunger.
The body is more affected by these evils
And the mind suffers many pains by mere contagion.
But if it were useful to it to make a body
One does not see any way that it could be done.
We can take it souls do not make bodies or parts of them,
Nor find their way into completed bodies,
Because if they did the connections would not be fine enough
For any common sensations to be established.

And why do fury and violence breed in the lion
As cunning does in foxes? And why is the flight of the stag
Inherited like the tremor that shakes his limbs?
And so with everything else, how is it that qualities
Go with the body and mind from the beginning
If not because there is a power in the seed
So that what is bred in grows as the body grows?
If it were immortal and went from body to body,
Then living creatures would be of changeable habits:
The fiercest kind of dogs would go running from stags,
The hawk would tremble at the approach of the dove,
And men would sniff around while the animals reasoned.

There is false logic behind the assertion
That immortal souls will change with a change of bodies.
For what is changed is dissolved and therefore perishes.
The parts are rearranged in a different order:
So they must be dissolved and spread through the whole
frame
And in the end perish when the body perishes.
If the argument is that human souls go always
Into human bodies, how is it, I ask you, the wise ones
Become so foolish, and why does no child have prudence?
And why is a foal less trained than a full-grown horse?
Is it not that in every seed and in every breed
There is a force of mind which grows up with the body?
Perhaps in a tender body the mind becomes tender?
But if it does, you cannot avoid the conclusion

That the soul is mortal, since in a different body
It loses so much of its former life and sense.

How could it possibly grow as it does with the body
And with it attain the lovely flower of its age
If it were not tied to the body from the beginning?
Or why should it want to escape when the body grows old
If it did not fear to be caught in an odious structure
And to find it fall to pieces, worn down with the years?
There would be no danger for an immortal soul.

Is it not absurd to suggest that at copulation
And the parturition of beasts the souls stand by,
Immortally anxious to get into mortal bodies,
Pushing and shoving, to see who can get in first?
Unless of course there is some agreement between them
That the first to come fluttering along has the right of entry,
Which would no doubt serve to relieve the confusion a little.

A tree cannot live in the air nor clouds in the sea,
Nor does one see fish enjoying themselves in fields;
There is no blood in wood, stones are quite without sap.
It is fixed and laid down where each thing has its habitat:
So the mind cannot come into being without a body
Nor can it exist far away from nerves and blood.
For if it could, then one might say *a fortiori*
It could exist in the head or shoulders or heels
And might be born into any part of the body,
So long as it was in the same man and the same container.
But since in our bodies too it is firmly laid down
Where the soul and mind can grow and have their existence
There cannot possibly be the slightest foundation
For saying they can exist outside the body.
And so, when the body dies, it must be admitted
The soul goes too in the same decomposition.

Indeed, to join the mortal and the eternal
And suppose that they can have feelings and actions in
                                                    common
Is imbecile. For what could be more incongruous,
Or what could be more disjointed and inconsistent
Than something mortal joined on to something immortal,
The two of them facing together the same cruel tempests?

Or is one perhaps to talk of the soul as immortal
Because it is protected from mortal dangers?
Or things which threaten its safety do not approach it?
Or because those which do are somehow forced to withdraw
Before we become aware of the harm they do?
That seems a long way off from the truth.
For besides the fact that the mind grows sick with the body
It is often tortured by the thoughts of the future
And suffers fear and is worn out by anxiety,
Besides being bitten by remorse for its faults.
Add to this madness and the loss of memory
And add that it sinks into dark floods of lethargy.

So death is nothing, and matters nothing to us
Once it is clear that the mind is mortal stuff.
And as in the time gone by we felt no ill
When the Carthaginians poured from all sides on us
And everything shaken by the tumult of war
Bristled and trembled under the bay of the sky
And everyone was in doubt to which contestant
Would fall the domination of land and sea:
So when we are dead and when our body and soul
Which together make us one, have come apart,
Nothing can happen to us, we shall not be there,
Nothing whatever will have the power to move us,
Not even if earth and sea got mixed into one.

And if our mind and soul after all do feel
When they have once been severed from the body,
It is nothing to us, for whom the bringing together
Of body and mind is the thing that makes us whole.
If time should collect up all our matter again
After our death, and put it back in position
So that once again we were given the light of life,
It would not concern us in any way at all
Once the line of recollection had been broken.
And now it does not concern us to know what we were;
Nor is it anything for us to worry about
What time should do with our substance in the future.
If you look backwards as it were across the distance
Of all past time, and think what great variety
There is in the movements of matter, you may well imagine

That the elements have often been placed as they are now;
But what those things out of which we are made were like
Is something our memories cannot at all recapture.
Life has been interrupted and all the wandering
Movements have taken place far away from our senses.

A man who is going to suffer any evil
Must live in the time when it is going to happen.
Death precludes this when it removes from the scene
The one on whom misfortunes are converging;
That shows that we have nothing to fear from death;
Nothing can happen to the man who is not there;
It is just the same as if he had never been born
When immortal death has taken his mortal life.

So when you see a man who grows indignant
That after death he will either rot away
Or be destroyed by flames or by wild beasts
You may say his voice sounds false, and that he is feeling
Some secret prick at his heart, although he pretends
To think he will be insensible after death,
He does not, to my mind, give as good as he promises
Or take himself up by the roots and right out of life
But unconsciously thinks that there must be something left.
A living man who imagines that after death
Vultures will eat him or wild beasts tear him up,
Takes pity upon himself: he does not distinguish
Sufficiently between himself and his corpse,
Imagining another self with his sensibility
And so he bewails that he was created mortal
Although in real death there would be no second self
Alive to regret that the first self was dead
Or to stand by while the corpse is bitten or burnt.
For if it is bad after death to be eaten by animals
I cannot see that it would not also be painful
To be put on the fire and so consumed by flames
Or stifled in honey, or to grow stiff with cold,
Lying upon a slab of freezing stone
Or to feel a load of earth weigh down upon you.

'— Yet there will be no pleasant house to go to,
Your wife and children will not be there to kiss you

98

And fill your heart with so much silent sweetness;
Nor will you any more be useful to them
By your successes. Unlucky', they say, you are
'For one unfortunate day will have taken the lot.'
They do not however add: 'Nor will you want anything,
There is no craving for anything after death.'
But if they realized this and followed it up
Their minds would be released from apprehension.
'You, as you now are in the sleep of death, will remain
For the rest of time, free from all pains and evils:
But we who, standing by your funeral pyre,
Mourn you insatiably, no time will ever
Take away from us this eternal grief.'
But, one might ask, what is there that is so bitter
In this coming in the end to sleep and rest?
How can anyone mourn eternally for that?

There are those who, when they take their place at table
And take a cup and put laurels round their heads,
Say from the heart: 'This pleasure will not last;
It will soon be over and we shall never have it again.'
As if in death they would be preoccupied
With the thought that they felt themselves extremely thirsty
Or indeed with any other regret whatever.

Nobody misses himself or the life he leads
When both his mind and body have fallen asleep:
For all we care that sleep might be everlasting,
There is no trace of any regret for ourselves:
And yet in sleep the elements have not left us
Or wandered away from contact with the senses
And when the man awakes he collects himself.
Death must therefore concern us less than sleep
If anything can be less than nothing is.
Much greater confusion in the material elements
Follows at death, and nobody wakes again
When once the chilling interval has occurred.

If nature found a voice and began to scold
This is the sort of thing she might say to any of us:
'What is all this fuss about because you are mortal?
Have you got to burst into tears? What is wrong with death?

If the life you have had so far has been quite pleasant
And everything has not gone down the drain with a rush,
Why not depart like a guest who has had enough?
And, you fool, take your simple rest with a quiet mind?
But if all the pleasures of life have turned to nothing
And life is offensive, why do you want to add to it
Days which will end as badly as those you have had?
Better to make an end of life and effort
For there is nothing new I can devise for you
That is likely to please you: the rest of life is the same.
If your body is not worn out and there is still some movement
In your arms and legs, still, nothing will ever change
Although you should go on living for several centuries
Or even supposing you did not die at all.'

What could we reply but that nature has a good case
And that as she presents it every word is true?
If some poor wretch should complain of death more than
                                                   he should
It serves him right if nature speaks even more sharply:
'No more blubbering, you moron; forget your complaints.'
And if it is a man of considerable age:
'You have gone feeble after having your life?
You want what you haven't got and despise the present
And that is how your life has slipped away.
Now death stands at your pillow before you are ready,
You cannot leave because you've not had enough!
You are too old for everything; give it up!
Give way gracefully; you have to, anyway.'

Perfectly right, and perfectly right to scold so;
For the old is always pushed out to make way for the new;
And one thing is renewed at the expense of another:
Nobody ever ends in the pit of Tartarus;
The matter is needed for the new generations,
All of which go the same way when their life is over,
Those before you did so and others will follow.
So one thing will never cease to emerge from another
And life is for no one to keep but for all to use.

Now look back: all the time that ever existed
Before we were born, was nothing at all to us.

It is a mirror which nature holds up for us
To show us what it will be like after our death.
Is it very horrible? Is there anything sad in it?
Is it any different from sleep? It is more untroubled.

The things they say happen to us in Acheron
Happen all right, but they happen to us here.
There is no Tantalus, as the story is,
Scared stiff by the fear that a rock might fall on him.
But in this life an empty fear of the gods
Haunts men and they dread how their fortunes will fall.

There is no Tityos, pecked at by birds in Acheron;
They could never find enough to eat on him
To last them, as is supposed, for all eternity,
However big you may imagine his body,
Not covering a mere nine acres with his limbs.
But even supposing they spread over the whole earth,
Still he could not suffer an everlasting pain
Or provide food for ever out of his own body.
But Tityos is here with us; he is the lover
Whose heart is eaten alive, that is anguish enough;
Or a man cut up by any other desire.

Sisyphus too is before us in this life.
He is the man who is always asking the people
For the rods and axes and always withdrawing defeated.
For seeking power is an empty request;
It is never given; to spend all your effort on that
Is just like pushing a heavy stone uphill
And down it comes as soon as it gets to the top;
It finds its way back to the level as soon as it can.

Always to be feeding an ungrateful mind,
Filling it with good things and never satisfying it
As the seasons fill us as they come round each year;
They bring their fruits and other delightful things
Though we are never filled with what life can give us:
This is like those girls who, in the flower of their age,
It is said spend their time pouring water through a sieve
Which in the nature of things can never be filled.

The furies, Cerberus, Tartarus in utter blackness
Eructating a horrible fire from its mouth,
Are things which never were and never will be:
But there is fear of penalties in this life,
The most notable penalties for the most notable crimes,
As prison, beatings, hot irons, racks and fires:
Even if it does not come to this, there is conscience,
Afraid to the point that it feels goaded and whipped
And does not see any end to the ills it suffers
And thinks that the punishments will go on for ever
And that after death they will be even more than he fears:
So the life of fools becomes a hell in itself.

This you may also usefully say to yourself:
The great king Ancus came to the end of his days
And he was a better man by far than you are.
And many other important people have died
Who exercised a great political influence,
Even Xerxes, who threw a bridge of boats over Hellespont
And so enabled his legions to go over dry-shod
As if a large and salty sea were nothing to him
And his cavalry could treat it with scorn, for all its roars:
He died, and his soul escaped the way they all do.
Scipio, a martial thunderbolt and terror of Carthage,
Left his bones to the earth like the meanest slave.
So too the inventors of the arts and sciences,
The artists and poets, of whom Homer was chief
And yet he has gone to find his sleep with the others.
Then Democritus: when old age gave its warnings
And he found that his memory had begun to fail,
He went to meet death of his own volition.
Epicurus died at the end of his brilliant life,
A man who was of more than human intellect,
Who put out the stars as the sun does at its rising.

Yet you hesitate and think it hard to die,
You who are half-dead while you are still alive?
Who pass the larger part of your life in sleep?
Who snore when you are awake and never stop dreaming?
Whose mind is exacerbated by pointless terrors?
Who do not know what is wrong with you, as often as not?

102

A wretched man drunk with all kinds of troubles,
Wandering around with a mind which is always in error.

If men, who seem to feel a weight upon them
As if their minds were worn out with a burden,
Could know the causes from which arises
So great a heap of trouble in their hearts,
They would not live as we see men generally do,
Not knowing what they want and always in search
Of some new place where they can lay their burden down.

A man may rush out of a magnificent palace
Because he is sick of the place, then go straight back
Because he feels no better anywhere else.
He drives like mad to reach his country house
As if he were going there to put out a fire
And yawns immediately he reaches the door;
Or falls into heavy sleep, to try to forget;
He may even hurry back again into town.
So everyone runs away from himself: but as this is impossible
In the end he has to put up with the man he hates;
He is sick and does not know the cause of his sickness:
If he understood it, he would put aside everything else
And spend his time entirely in studying nature
For what is in question is not a moment of time
But the state in which he will pass eternity,
The ages which wait for mortals after death.

And why should we tremble so in doubts and dangers?
What evil desire for life constrains us to it?
The end of mortal life is something certain;
There is no other way with death but to meet it.
We turn around in a circle and there we are
And no new place is to be got by living.
Yet what we haven't got and would not like to have
Seems marvellous: we get it and want something else
And so the thirst for life will keep us running
Although it is uncertain what the future holds,
What luck we shall have or what our end will be.

By protracting life we cannot reduce one iota
The time we shall spend in death; we have not the power

To give ourselves any less annihilation.
Bury as many generations as you like,
Eternal death is still what waits for you;
It will be no less for the man who dies today
Than it is for the man who died months or years ago.

BOOK IV

The poet describes his novel mission, of making philosophy pleasant. He goes on to explain how images are given off from objects, their formation and the speed of their movements. This leads him to the subject of sensation, its causes, the false inferences the mind may draw, and the infallibility of the senses themselves. He then treats of the processes of thought, and dreams. He considers some functions of the body and their relationships with the mind and will, and so comes to the origin of love, which is of course physical. Then follows the famous attack on the passion of love.

I wander over so many trackless places
No poet has been in before: I approach new springs
And drink them up: and I like to pick new flowers
To make an unusual wreath about my head:
First, because my subject is important,
Nothing less than an attempt to get rid of religion;
Then because I make the most lucid verses
From obscure material and give it the grace of poetry.
There is, I may say, an excellent reason for that.
When doctors are giving children a bitter medicince
They first of all will smear the rim of the cup with honey
And in that way the sweet and golden liquid
Deceives the children at least as far as their lips
And so they swallow down the bitter substance;
You may say they are beguiled but hardly misled
Since by these means they recover health and strength:
So I now, since this doctrine is rather repugnant
To those not exercised in it, and for most people
Something they would not touch, I wanted to put it
With all the agreeableness there can be in verse
And as it were smear it with poetical honey
To see if I could keep your mind on my verses
Until you understood the order of nature
And felt the usefulness of what I am saying.

I have already explained the nature of mind,
Its composition and how it works in the body
And how when detached it returns to its first elements.

Now I will start on another subject, closely
Connected with it: the existence of images
Which are like membranes from the surface of things;
Once torn off they flutter here and there in the air,
And it is they which alarm us when they encounter our
                                              waking
Minds, as they do in dreams, when we often see strange
                                              shapes
And the images of those who have lost the light
Rouse us in horror as we lie powerless in sleep.
We should not think they are souls escaped from Acheron
Or ghosts which are wandering around among living men,
Nor that any part of us can be left after death
When the body and mind have been destroyed together
And both resolved once more into their elements.

What I am saying is that representations, filmy shapes
Are sent off all the time from the surface of things
— Something like membranes or you might call it a rind
Since it has the appearance and form of the thing itself —
These things wander away from the body they come from.

I think I can demonstrate this even to the stupidest:
First, it can be directly observed in many cases.
There are things that give off emanations which spread,
As smoke from burning wood or heat from fire;
There are others where what is given off is denser,
As the casings the cicadas shed in summer
And the membranes calves drop from around their bodies
When they are born; or the skin which slippery snakes
Leave hooked on thorns, so that we often see
Briars hung about with these fluttering trophies.
Since these things happen, it must be that a thin image
Is given off from the surface of things.
For why these things should fall in the way they do
But not the really thin films, is not demonstrable:
Especially since there are on the surface of bodies
Many small particles, which could remain in the order
They were in before, and entirely keep their shape,
And come off more quickly since there is little to stop them
As they are, so to speak, in the very first line of particles.

106

We certainly see a number of things given off
Not only from within, as I said before,
But from the surface of things, as happens with colour:
You see how yellow and red and steely blue awnings,
Stretched over theatres and billowing over the beams,
Dye all the auditorium and those in it,
The scene itself, the senators, matrons, the gods,
Making them all so to speak swim in the colour;
And indeed the more they are shut in by high walls,
The more everything is gay in the rarefied light.
As the canvas gives the colouring off from its surface
So everything must give off a thin film of likeness,
The surface in every case producing a discharge
And there are always shreds of appearances
Fluttering about in the air, in a form so impalpable
That they cannot be distinguished in the ordinary way.

On the other hand smell, smoke, heat and other such matters
Pour out of things and are at the same time dissipated
Because since they come from somewhere deep down in
                                                    the object
They are split up on the way: there is no clear route
And no way out in which they could keep together.
But of course when a membrane of superficial colour
Is thrown off there is nothing which could break it up
Since it is in the first rank and ready to go.

Finally, with mirrors, water, all shiny surfaces
In which there appear to us images of objects
They perfectly represent, it must be the case
That they are made of skins which come from the objects
                                                    themselves.

There are therefore likenesses of things, thin forms
Which nobody can discern, taken one at a time,
But which, when they are thrown off one after another,
Reflect from a mirror something which can be seen;
There does not seem to be any other way in which
Appearances could be perfectly reproduced.

Now see how slight is the nature of the image.
The first point is that the elements of things

Are very much smaller than our senses perceive
Not immediately below the threshold of our vision.
In order to make this clear, I will try to indicate
Briefly how tenuous the elements really are.

Consider first a minute creature, of which a third part
Would not be visible to the sharpest sight.
How big do you suppose its intestines would be?
Or its heart or its eyes? Or any limb or joint?
How tiny must they be? Yet think of the elements
Of which its soul and mind must be constructed!
How extremely near to nothing they must be!

Again, those things which give off pungent odours
As various herbs do, such as bitter absinth,
Strong-scented southernwood and sharp centaury.
Take one of these and press between your fingers . . .
But what you should know is that the images wander
Here and there with no power to affect the senses.

But do not suppose the only wandering images
Are those thrown off by natural objects;
There are others which you may call self-generated,
Formed in the sky or rather in the air;
These take shape variously and are carried aloft
And are fluid enough continually to change shape:
They take indeed one outline after another,
As clouds which are easy to see gathering on high
Until they break up the blue stretch of the sky,
Sliding along through the air: the faces of giants
Are seen in flight above us and bring their shadows;
Then great mountains and great rocks torn from mountains
March through the air and pass across the sun;
Then monsters come and bring with them more
                                        storm-clouds.

How easily and swiftly images are generated,
Flowing from things all the time, and slipping away.
The surface of objects is always giving off something
Which is thrown out: and when it meets certain substances
Such as glass, it passes through: but with rock
Or such material as wood, it is torn up at once

And in these cases it cannot give back an image.
But when it meets a substance shiny and close-packed,
A mirror especially, nothing of this sort happens.
It cannot pass through as with cloth, nor yet get torn.
The polished surface recalls it in its entirety.
And so it is such surfaces send back images,
Suddenly as you like, in less than no time.
Hold a thing up to a mirror, the image appears;
Which shows that tenuous material and tenuous shapes
Are constantly being given off from the surface of things.
That is why images are produced so quickly,
You can call that quick if you can call anything so.
And just as the sun takes little time to produce
A mass of sunbeams, so that the world is full of them,
In the same way, in a moment of time,
Innumerable images must be carried from everything
In a number of ways and out in every direction;
That is why whichever way we turn the mirror
It gives back things of similar form and colour.

And then, you may observe how a perfect sky
May suddenly be made turbid in every direction,
As if all the shadows had fled from Acheron
To fill the enormous caverns of the day;
So much, when the black night of clouds has gathered,
Hang over us all the faces of terrible fear.
How small a part is the image which appears to us
Of all that is there, impossible to say.

And now: how swiftly are these images carried,
How mobile they are as they cross the sky;
In a short time they are miles away
In whatever direction the spirit takes them.
I will say this in verses delectable rather than numerous:
For the swan's short song sounds better than all the noise
The cranes make scattered among the clouds of the south.

First then, light things, and those made of tiny particles,
Seem almost always things which move with speed;
An example is the light or heat of the sun:
Because these are made up of tiny elements
Which are so to speak pushed through the intervening air

By a series of shocks which follow in rapid succession,
Light is followed at once by further light,
Each flash driven on by the one behind.
Images must be supposed, in a similar manner,
To travel vast distances in a moment of time.
They do so partly because they have at their back
A tiny stimulus which sends them forward
And partly because they are made of such loose material
That they can easily penetrate what they meet;
It is as if they went through the gaps in the air.

And then, if particles which are given out
From deep inside objects, such as the light of the sun
And its heat, are able in an instant of time
To spread themselves across the whole space of the sky,
To fly across sea and land, and flood the sky,
What shall we say of those which lie on the surface,
When they are thrown off, nothing stands in their way;
Do you not see that they must go faster and further,
Traversing distances much greater than those
Which the sun's rays could traverse in the same time.

Here is another example from which you can see
Plainly with what velocity images travel:
As soon as a sheet of water is exposed to the night,
If the stars are shining, then you will see instantaneously
The constellations reflected in the water.
You see in how brief a moment an image
Falls from the edge of the universe down to the ground.

All this is one more proof that things emit particles
Which strike on the eyes and so give rise to vision;
From some things there is a constant flow of smells,
Coolness from rivers, heat from the sun, and from the sea,
                                                spray
Which eats into walls placed on the seashore,
And a mixture of sounds is always in the air;
A wet salt taste comes often on our lips
When we walk by the sea; and if we watch
Wormwood being prepared, the bitterness works on us.
So true is it that something is given off from everything
And ceaselessly carried away in all directions:

There is never any pause for these emanations;
We feel them all the time and we are for ever
Seeing or smelling, feeling or hearing something.

And since an object we handle in the dark
Is known to be the same as the object we see
In the brightest light of day, it must be the case
That one and the same cause produces touch and sight.
For example if we feel something square in the dark
What can it be which falls to our view in the light
Except an image of that same square thing?
Images must therefore be what cause us to see
And it is clear nothing can be seen without them.

These images I am talking about are carried
In all directions, they are projected everywhere:
It is true that because we see only with our eyes
It is only in the direction we turn our looks to
That things will strike us with their form and colour.
It is also the image which makes it possible
For us to see how far away anything is.
When it leaves an object, it pushes before it
The air which is between the object and our eyes;
It flows across the surface of our eyes
So to speak brushing the pupils, and passes on.
It is in that way that we are enabled to see
How far away anything is; the more air is pushed our way
And the longer the column of air which brushes our eyes
The further away will the object seem to be.
Admittedly all this happens at high velocity,
So that when we see something, we see how distant it is.

It is not an objection to this theory
That the images which strike upon our eyes
Cannot be separately seen, though the objects are seen.
It is as when a wind blows hard against us
Or sharp cold flows about us, we do not feel
Each several particle of wind or of cold
But rather the general effect: we have the sensation
Of a succession of blows upon our body
As if they were inflicted by a body outside it.
So when we tap a stone with our fingers, we touch

111

The outside of the rock, its surface and colour;
But that is not what touch conveys to us, rather
We feel hardness running deep into the rock.

Why does an image seen in a mirror appear
Beyond it? It does in fact seem deep within it.
It is as when we see real things outside the house
Through open doors which leave our view unobstructed
Enabling various objects out there to be seen.
Two lots of air are in play in what is seen.
First there is that between the eye and the door;
Then come the leaves of the door to left and right
And then the outside light sweeps over the eyes
With the second lot of air from the things outside.

So with the image which comes to us from a mirror;
As it comes to our sight it drives before it the air
Which is between itself and our eyes; the effect
Is that we are able to become aware of all this
Before we are aware of the mirror. When we do perceive that
An image from us is carried from us to the mirror
And in reflection comes back again to our eyes
Pushing another lot of air in front of it,
And we see this before we see it, which has the effect
That it seems to be at a distance from the mirror.
So there is as you may see no cause for wonder
That images give back what is seen from the mirror's
                                                    surface
In the way they do; two lots of air are in play.

And if in the mirror the right side of the body
Appears on the left, it is because when the image
Strikes on the mirror's surface it does not rebound
Without having undergone change: what happens is this,
It turns inside out, as would happen with a plaster mask
If, before it was dry, someone slapped it against a pillar
And it somehow preserved the lines of the features in front
And was pressed backwards as it received the shock;
It would happen that the right eye became the left
And conversely what had been the left eye would be the
                                                    right.

It can happen that an image is carried from mirror to mirror
So that there are five or six reflections of one object.
Things which were hiding behind a mirror, or in some
Tortuous recess, however out of the way,
Are all brought out by the repeated reflection;
It is the play of the mirror which brings them to light.
So the image is repeated from mirror to mirror,
What was left in the object becomes at first the right
And at the next reflection is true left again.

There are concave mirrors which curve to our sides,
These send back the image of our right hand to the right;
Either because it is only after a double reflection
That the image comes to us, or else because
On the way to us it makes a turn in the air
In response to the curvature of the mirror it came from.

You would think that images step out and put their foot
                                                    down
At the same time as we do, and imitate our movements.
When you withdraw from any part of the mirror
Images forthwith cease to issue from it;
It is natural with all things that the angle of recoil
Should be identical with the angle of incidence.

Bright things trouble the eyes, which therefore seek to
                                              avoid them:
The sun may even blind if you fix your gaze upon it,
Both because its own force is so great and because the
                                                  images
Coming from it fall heavily through the clear air,
Striking the eyes and upsetting the connections inside them.
A very bright light will sometimes burn the eyes
Because it contains the elements of fire,
Many of them, and so will cause pain to the eyes.
Things that the jaundiced look at appear to be yellow;
Elements of yellow flowing from the body
Encounter the images which come from objects;
Many such elements are mixed in the eyes themselves
And so paint everything with their pallid contagion.

When in the dark we can see things which are in the light
Because, as the air that is in the darkness is nearer

113

It gets to us first and fills our open eyes;
The brightly lighted air follows it immediately
And so to speak cleans out our eyes and scatters the shadows
Of the first lot of air: for it is a great deal more mobile,
The elements are smaller, and it works more effectively.
As soon as it has filled our eyes with light,
Opening the passages which the dark air has stopped,
The images of things in the light come immediately
And stimulate our eyes and so we see.
This does not however work the other way round;
When in the light we cannot see things in the dark
For then the thicker air of darkness comes second,
Stops all the openings and blocks our ocular passages
So that images cannot reach the eyes to move them.
When we see far off the square towers of a town
It often happens that they appear to us round;
Any angle seen from far away looks obtuse
Or not like an angle at all: the impact it gives
Dies on the way and nothing of it reaches our eyes,
The images coming to us through so much air
Are beaten about by the air and become less sharp.
When all the angles have thus eluded perception
It is as if the tower had been turned on a wheel,
Not like something at hand which is really round
But rather with the outline sketched in a shadowy way.

Our shadow seems also to move in the sunshine,
To follow our footsteps and imitate our gestures;
(Do you think that air which is deprived of light
Can step out and follow the movements and actions of men?
For it can be nothing more than air without light,
That which we are accustomed to call our shadow.)
Particular bits of the ground are deprived of light
Successively, as we move around in the world
And the area we leave is correspondingly filled;
That explains why the shadow cast by our body
Appears to follow us from place to place.
All the time there are new rays pouring in
And the old disappear, like wool spun into the fire.
In the same way the whole earth is drained of light
And filled again and so washes away its shadows.

It is not a question of our eyes being deceived.
Their function is to observe where the light falls
And where there is shadow: but whether all lights are the
same
And whether it is the same shadow, now here, now there
Or whether things are not rather as we have explained them,
That is a matter for the mind to determine:
It is not for the eyes to find out the working of nature;
Don't blame them for what the mind ought to be doing.

The ship which carries us seems to be standing still;
The one which remains at her moorings seems to move;
And hills and fields seem to fall back astern
When it is we who are driving ahead under sail.
All the stars seem at rest and fixed in the caves of the sky
Yet they never cease to move; they rise and set
And move across vast distances in between
Having measured out the sky with their brilliant light.
In the same way the sun and moon look as if they stand still
And yet it is perfectly clear that they are moving.
Mountains which rise up far away at sea
May be divided by straits which admit great fleets
Though it looks as if they were parts of a single island.
The atrium seems to turn and the columns run round,
To children when they stop turning themselves: and they
almost
Believe that the roof is coming down on their heads.

At dawn, when nature begins to raise the glow
Of brilliant, tremulous beams across the mountains,
It seems to you the sun is on top of the mountains,
As if it were touching them with its brilliant fire;
Yet the hills are hardly two thousand bow-shots from us;
They may perhaps be as little as five hundred;
And between them and the sun lie all the vast stretches
Of sea, beneath immense tracts of the ether;
And in between are many thousands of lands
Inhabited by many races and wild beasts.

On the other hand, a simple puddle of water,
Standing between the paving-stones in the road,
Offers a view stretching underneath the earth

115

As far as the sky does in the other direction
So that you see the clouds and the sky
Withdrawn far into that sky below the earth.

And then, when our horse stands stock-still in a river
And we look downwards into the flowing water
The body of the horse seems to be carried upstream
Although he is standing still with the water against him
And wherever we turn our eyes all we see is carried
Or seems to be, the same way as ourselves.

A portico which runs in parallel lines,
Supported all along by equal columns,
If it is long and we look from one end to the other,
Seems gradually to draw out into a long cone,
The roof touching the ground, the right the left,
So that the eye loses itself at the vanishing point.

At sea, it seems to sailors that the sun
Rises and sets in the waves and buries its light in them;
Because they observe nothing but water and sky;
But do not suppose the senses are generally shaky.
To those who know nothing of the sea it seems
A ship in harbour is broken below the waterline
With the lower parts pressing up against the surface.
The part of the oars above the water is straight
And so is the upper part of the stern of the ship;
The parts under water look as if they are bent,
Broken, turning back to the horizontal;
They almost float back to the surface of the water.

When scattered clouds are driven across the heavens
During the night, it seems that the glittering stars
Are moving against the clouds and travelling aloft
In a direction quite different from their real one.

If you press with your hand the lower part of one eye
The effect upon your vision is that you see
Everything in its range as if it were double;
A double flame blazing from all the torches
And all the furniture in the house looks double
And men have double faces and double bodies.

And when we are entirely given over to sleep
And our body is lying still in completest quiet,
We may seem to ourselves to be awake and to move
Ourselves about; and in the darkness of night
We think we see the sun and the light of day
And, shut in our room, find fresh seas, skies, rivers
And mountains and to be walking over fresh fields,
To hear sounds and, when the severe silence of night
Is everywhere, to speak although we are silent.

There are many other phenomena of this kind
Which threaten the credibility of our senses:
Or seem to, for in fact they are for the most part
Due to the judgement which we have added ourselves
So that we seem to see what in fact we do not see.
Nothing is harder than to distinguish between
Patent facts and the doubts which the mind contributes.

Anyone who thinks that nothing is known
On his own admission cannot assert even that.
I do not think it worth arguing a case
Against a man who is standing on his head.
But let us suppose he does know nothing is known;
I would ask him, since he has seen no truth in anything,
How he can know what knowing and not knowing are?
What are the marks of truth and the marks of falsehood?
How can one tell the doubtful from the certain?
You will find that it is the senses which first created
The criterion of truth, they cannot be shown to be wrong:
Credibility must attach to whatever
Makes it possible to set aside the false for the true.
What has more credibility than the senses?
Is it possible that a reason based on lying senses
Should contradict them, since it is them she comes from?
If they are not true, then reason itself is a lie.
Can the ears correct the eyes? Or the touch the ears?
Can the sense of taste question the sense of touch?
Can the nose refute it? Or the eyes say it is false?
I do not think so: every sense has its function
Each can do something the others cannot do.
One perceives hardness or softness, cold or heat;
Another perceives the variety of colours

117

And the qualities which go together with colour.
Taste has its particular sense; smell has another,
And it is the same with sound; and so it must be
That no one sense can ever convince another,
Nor can a particular sense correct itself
Since it is as credible at one time as another.
What any sense perceives anywhere is true.

If reason cannot, for example, find out the cause
Why an object which, close at hand, appears to be square,
Looks round at a distance, it is very much better
To try to explain it by a false hypothesis
Than to deny the manifest facts of the case,
To go against evidence and so tear up the foundations
On which our life and our safety must depend.
Not only would reason go down in the ruin;
Life itself would fall if you dared not trust the senses
To keep you away from precipices and such dangers
And to show you the sort of things that you can rely on;
So all that talk is absolutely vain
Which seeks to ruin the credit of the senses.

In any building, if the basic measure is wrong
And there is error in judging the perpendicular
Or the level somewhere is even the slightest bit wrong,
Everything will be out of true and lopsided,
Crooked, sloping, leaning this way or that;
It will threaten to fall and some of it actually will fall
And all on account of the first erroneous measurements:
So your reasoning about things is always bound to be false
If it is based on senses you cannot rely on.

The way in which the senses perceive their several objects
Must now be explained; it is not a difficult matter.
First, voices and sounds of every kind are heard
When they enter the ears and strike the appropriate organs;
And sounds and voices must be allowed to be physical
Because they do in fact strike on the senses.
Moreover the voice will often scrape the throat
And a shout will roughen the channels it passes through.
That is because the elements of sound
Are bunched in a passage which is too narrow for them

And cannot get through into the air outside
Without some damage to the exit they make use of.
So there can be no doubt that voices and words consist
Of physical elements or they could not cause injury.
You must have noticed how physically exhausting
It is, how much nervous energy it uses,
When one has to talk without ceasing from dawn to nightfall,
Especially if you have to talk at the top of your voice.
So it must be admitted that the voice is physical
Since a man by much talking loses part of his body.

The roughness of the voice will come from the roughness
Of the elements, as the smoothness comes from the
                                                    smoothness.
The elements which reach the ears are not the same
When the barbarian trumpet calls like a bull and re-echoes
As when swans from the cool valleys of Helicon
Rain their liquid voices in mournful complaint.
When we express our voices from the depth of the body
And send them out into the world through the mouth
The tongue will twist and fashion them into words
And the lips too have their part in giving them shape.
When the distance is not long between the starting-point
And the point to which the voice goes, the words can be
                                                    heard
Plainly and every syllable is articulate;
The fashioning and the shape are then preserved.
But if the space between the two is too great
The words are confused in passing through so much air
And in its flight the voice is troubled and muddied.
Then you get a sound you can hear, but you cannot
                                                    distinguish
One word from another or gather the meaning:
So thrown awry and obstructed is the voice.

Sometimes a single word will strike the ears
Of a crowd of people, as when the crier shouts:
That means that a single voice has been divided,
Spread instantaneously among a thousand ears,
Stamping upon them the clear sound of the word.

But the parts of voices which do not fall upon ears
Die and are carried pointlessly through the air;

Some strike on solid things and the sound comes back
And we are deceived by the image of the word.
When you understand that, you can easily explain
To yourself and others how in empty places
The rocks throw back the sound of words in order,
As we seek our friends wandering among dark mountains
And loudly call where we know them to be scattered.

I have known places give back six or seven voices
When you tossed them one: so hills give back to hills,
Repeating from one to another the words they have learned.
These are places the nymphs and satyrs inhabit
Or so the inhabitants say, and they speak of fauns
Whose noises in the night and boisterous play
Break up, so they say, the most silent nights;
And they hear the sound of strings, and sweet complaints
Pour forth from pipes as the players' fingers touch them;
For the country people this is the sound of Pan,
Shaking the crown of pine on his half-wild head
As he runs his curved lip over the open reeds
And pours out woodland songs. More of this kind
Of marvels and portents they will treat you to;
They do not want you to think them the only people
Who live in places which the gods have deserted,
And so they boast of the miracles they can tell of,
Not least, perhaps, because like other people
They like to have someone to listen to what they say.

We need not be astonished that barriers of a kind
Which do not allow us to see things plainly through them
Allow the passage of voices which we can hear:
Nothing more common than talking through a door.
The explanation is that a voice can travel
Through space in things which images could not pass;
They are torn if they cannot travel in a straight line
As they can do through the interstices of glass.

Besides, a voice is divided in all directions;
One sound produces another, and when one has started
It flies apart and multiplies, as a spark
Will scatter, becoming a thousand points of fire.
So places are filled with voices and places concealed

By objects all round them still vibrate with sound
But images always follow a direct line
From their point of origin; that is why no one can see
Through a wall though voices can easily pass through it.
Yet even a voice, going through the walls of a house,
Is dulled and reaches our ears in some confusion,
So we seem to hear not so much words as a sound.

The tongue and palate by which we can perceive flavours
May be explained without any greater difficulty.
First, flavours are perceived in the mouth, when we masticate
What we eat, pressing it like a spongeful of water
When someone starts to squeeze it in his hand,
Then what we press out goes through the pores of the palate
And finds its way through the intricacies of the tongue.
When the elements of the trickling flavour are smooth
The contact is pleasant and there is a pleasant tickling
Around the moistening areas of the mouth.
But the elements bite and tear the organs of sense
More as they have more of roughness in them.

The pleasure of tasting things ends at the palate:
When once whatever provokes it has gone down the throat,
There is no pleasure, it simply spreads round the body:
It does not matter then what you have been fed on
So long as you can digest whatever it is
And it serves to keep the stomach moist as it should be.

I will now explain how it is that different foods
Suit different creatures; and what seems disagreeable
And bitter to one may seem sweet to another.
There are such great disparities in this matter
That what is food to one, to another is poison.
A snake for example will die if human saliva
Touches him; he will bite himself to pieces.
And again, for us, hellebore is a poison
Yet goats and quail grow fat enough upon it.
To understand how such things come about
You have to remember what I have told you already,
That different things have different mixtures of elements.
All living creatures which are dependent on food
Have different outward appearances; breed by breed,

They are of different shapes on the outside
Because they consist of elements of different shapes.
And since they differ in elements, necessarily,
There must be differences also in the pores
All over the body, not least in the mouth and palate.
Some of them must be smaller and some larger;
Some will be square and some of them triangular;
Many will be round, and some of them polygonal.
The shape and movement of elements will determine
The different shapes of the openings, and result in
Variety in the physiological texture.
That is why what is sweet to one is sour to another;
It is sweet to those through the pores of whose palates
                                        the smoothest
Elements can enter so as to press closely inside them.
On the other hand, the same thing may well taste sharp
To those whose throats the rough, hooked elements enter.

From this you can easily see how other things happen.
For example, where there is someone in a fever
Through excess of bile or through some other disease,
What happens is that the whole body is disturbed;
There are rearrangements in the position of elements:
Then things which hitherto have suited the senses
Suit them no longer, and others are more appropriate,
Which are able to find their way in and produce bitterness.
Both kinds of substance are to be found in honey,
A point I have made on a number of occasions.

Now let us get on to the subject of smells.
I will explain. First of all, there must be many things
From which there flows a varied stream of smells;
And no doubt they are spent and scattered everywhere.
But one smell finds itself more nearly adapted
To one group of creatures; it is a matter of structure.
Bees are attracted for miles by the smell of honey
And vultures by corpses: and dogs can follow a scent
Left behind by the track of a cloven hoof.
And human beings can be smelt at a distance
By the bird which saved the Capitol, the white goose.
So different scents lead different beasts to their food
And warn them off the things which will do them harm;
In this way the wild animals are preserved.

Of all the different smells which affect our nostrils
Some come from much greater distances than others
But none of them is carried so far as sound
May be, or a voice, and certainly not so far
As things which affect the eyes and so become visible.
Smell comes on wanderingly and slowly
And is quickly lost as it spreads itself in the air;
It comes from inside things and finds it hard to get out.
The fact that smells flow from interior parts
Is shown by the way that everything seems to give
A stronger smell when it is crushed and pounded.
This proves that smells are made of larger elements
Than voices; they will not penetrate stone walls
Through which voices and sounds will easily pass.
For this reason, with a smell, it is very difficult
To trace exactly where it has its origin;
It grows cold dawdling through the air, the informing
Elements are not warm when they arrive.
So dogs will often go wrong and miss the scent.
What I have said applies not only to smells
And flavours; the appearance of things, and colours
Are better fitted to some creatures' sight than others';
Some are even painful to certain eyes.
There is the cock, which flaps its wings in the morning
And crows in the dawn with so lucid a voice:
This is something the ferocious lion cannot face;
He cannot help himself but he thinks of flight:
The reason is that in the body of the cock
There are certain elements which, in the eyes of lions,
Bore into the pupils and cause the beasts such anguish
That for all their fierceness they cannot stand their ground,
Though when these elements strike upon our eyes
They do no damage, do not penetrate, or if they do,
Easily get out again, so they cannot by staying
Cause injury to any part of the eye.

Now let us talk about things which move the mind
And where they come from, I can explain it all.
First let me say, that there are many images
Wandering around, you might say, all over the place.
They are tenuous and readily joined together in the air
When they meet, like spiders' webs or gold leaf.

These things are of a far thinner texture
Than those which strike the eye and give rise to vision;
They come in through the porous parts of the body,
Touch the fine nature of the mind and make an impression.
That is how we come to see centaurs and bits of Scylla,
Dogs which look like Cerberus, and the images
Of those whose bones have long been underground.
All kinds of images are floating everywhere,
Some of them generated in the air itself,
Some having peeled off from the outside of things
And some made of a combination of both.
The centaurs' images cannot come from the life
Since there was never any such creature in nature.
When images of a horse and a man come together
They stick to one another, as I have shown.
An image of that kind makes an immediate impression
Upon our minds, which are themselves of material
Extremely tenuous and marvellous in its mobility.

This will show that my explanation is the correct one:
So far as what we see with the mind and the eyes
Is similar, it must have a similar origin.
I have shown that the reason I see, for example, a lion
Is that there are images which affect the eyes.
The mind must surely be moved in a similar way
By the image of the lion or of anything else,
Just like the eyes, though it sees more tenuous images.
It is for this reason that when we are deep in sleep
But the mind is awake, we are troubled by those images
Which stimulate our minds when we are awake;
To the point indeed that we seem to see
Those whom death has taken and earth now holds.
Nature does things in this way because the senses
With the rest of the body are put out of action
And so cannot check the false against the true;
And because the memory is also asleep
And does not remind us that the person we think we see
Has long been taken into the power of death.
No need to be surprised that the images move
Their arms and legs in time, as sometimes
Seems to happen with images seen in dreams.
For, as one image dies, another is born

In another position, and so we think there is movement;
Of course all this happens at incredible speed.

One could ask many questions about all this. There is
Much to explain if the matter is to be made clear.
In the first place one might ask why as soon as we want to
Think of anything the mind obliges and thinks of it.
Can it be that the images see what we are after
And, as soon as we want it, a particular image pops up?
If we are preoccupied by sea, earth or sky,
Assemblies, processions, banquets or maybe battles,
Does nature produce them at the appropriate word?
The remarkable thing is that people in one spot
May none the less be thinking of different things.

What about when in dreams we see images
Advancing in step and making flexible gestures,
Swinging their arms in turn and with rapidity
And going over the movement again and again?
A skilful set of images, you might say;
Perhaps they took lessons in order to entertain us?
Will not the truth be, that the instant we are aware of,
In which the voice can utter a single word,
Conceals other instants distinguishable by reason
And in any particular instant a number of images
Is ready at hand on the spot in case they are wanted?
So mobile are they, and so great is the stock of them.
And since they are tenuous, unless it tries to, the mind
Cannot see what is there; and the rest, which are not wanted,
Are lost, leaving only those which the mind has need of.
It prepares for what is coming, and hopes it will see
What ought to follow: and that is just what it does see.

Do you not see that our eyes, when they are trying
To make out something fine, deliberately strain
And that without that we cannot see so distinctly?
Even with things which are as plain as a pikestaff
There has to be some attention or else they will seem
All the time to be a long way away.
What wonder then if the mind loses sight of everything
Except the particular things it is attending to?

We are apt too, on the slightest indication,
To see great visions and so deceive ourselves.
It does not always happen that an image is followed
By another of the same kind, but what was a woman
Turns out when we touch to be a man
Or faces and ages change inconsequentially:
We are not astonished because of sleep and forgetfulness.

In matters of this kind there is a common fallacy
Which you should run away from as if it would scorch you:
You should not imagine that eyes were made to see with
Nor that the long steps we are able to take
Explain the origin of the feet and legs
And why they are jointed in the way they are;
Nor that the arms are so fixed on the shoulders
And a pair of useful hands hung at our sides
To enable us to use them as we do.

Such explanations are based on erroneous reasoning.
Nothing of all the bits which make up our body
Is there so that we can use it; the use is invented
By the mere fact that the organ or limb is there:
There was no seeing until the eyes were born
Nor was there speech before the tongue was created;
On the contrary, the tongue came a long time before speech;
The ears were invented before a sound was heard
And every organ, before it had any use.
So nothing came for the sake of the use we have found for it.

Yet obviously the habit of pugnaciousness,
Of breaking bones and spilling gallons of blood
Had not to await the invention of arrows and javelins
And nature suggested the avoidance of wounds
Before the left arm artfully held a shield;
The weary body would lay itself down to sleep
Before soft beds were made for it to sleep on
And slaking thirst is older than drinking from cups.
Such articles, answering our daily needs,
May well be thought to have been designed for use.
It is otherwise with the things which were first created
And later gave us ideas of how we might use them.
Of these the limbs and senses are good examples.

It is quite impossible to believe that they were
Created for us to use them as we do.
It is not to be wondered at that the body of every
Living creature is such that it looks for food.
I have shown that particles flow away from everything
In various ways: and most of all they must flow
From living creatures, always in restless motion.
Many particles come from inside, carried out by sweat;
Many out of the mouth, when the creatures pant with
                                                    fatigue.

In this way the body is rarefied, its very nature
Undermined, and there is consequent pain.
Therefore food is taken to keep it together,
To give it strength by diffusion through the veins:
This has the effect of stopping the craving to eat.

Liquid flows into every part of the body
Which calls for liquid, elements of warmth collect
And produce a kind of burning in the stomach
Which the advent of liquid extinguishes as it would fire
So that the burning can no longer consume us.
It is thus that a gasping thirst is washed away
And that a passionate hunger is satisfied.

Now how does it happen that we are able to walk
When we want to, and to make what movements we please?
And how do we manage to push our bodies about,
Heavy as they are? I will tell you: and you pay attention.
An image of walking presents itself to the mind
And strikes it in the manner I have explained.
This gives the will: there cannot be any action
Without the mind first determining what it wants,
Which happens only when the image presents itself.
When the mind has bestirred itself and decides on walking
A step is made, for at once throughout the body
The soul is struck by elements of the mind,
Which is easy enough, the two are so close together.
The soul then strikes on the body, and the whole bulk
Is stimulated and so put in motion.
The body relaxes its tissues so that the air,
A substance which is eternally on the move,
Comes into the openings, making its way through the pores

And spreads into the minutest parts of the body.
There are thus always these two causes in play
And the body moves like a ship with sails and wind.
There is, you will see, no occasion for astonishment
That such small elements can turn a body around
In spite of all its weight, for we know that the wind,
Subtle and fine as it is, can drive on a ship
And a single hand steer however great the speed,
And a single rudder turn it wherever you like.
So it is with pulleys and that sort of equipment;
You have machines which can raise things with hardly an
                                                 effort.

Now I will tell you how the waves of quiet
Flow through the mind in sleep and release it from care;
I will make the verses sweet and not too many
For the swan's little song is better than all the clamour
Of cranes blowing about in the clouds from the south.
Your ear should be finely tuned and your mind attentive
Or you may contradict and reject what I say
Although my words will all be perfectly true
And the fault will be yours if you do not see my point.

In the first place, sleep occurs when the soul is scattered,
Part of it being expelled from the body
And part of it pushed down far into the interior.
Then the limbs are relaxed and without resistance.
There is no doubt that it is by the soul that we feel
And when sleep hinders the senses we must suppose
That the soul is out of its course and perhaps expelled;
Not all of it, however, for if it were
The body would be caught in the chill of death.
If no part of the soul were left in the limbs
In the way that fire will lie hidden in ashes
How could our feelings suddenly break out again
As flames will rise up suddenly out of ash?

But how this change comes about and how it happens
That the soul can be put out and the body grow limp
Is something I will explain and you, I hope, listen to.

The surface of any body, in the first place,
Being next to the air is constantly in touch with it;

128

It is hammered all the time by the beating air.
That is why almost everything is covered with skin,
Or shells, or some hard substance or something like bark.
The inner part of every creature that breathes
Is also struck by the air pumped in and out.
So the body is beaten outside and inside alike
By blows which arrive by means of tiny apertures
At the elements of which the body is made
And gradually bring us into a state of ruin.
The arrangement of elements in both body and mind
Is in fact disturbed; one part of the soul is thrown out,
Another part hides itself in the innards,
And part is spread through the limbs and for this reason
                                                    cannot
Act in concert or feel the effects of a movement:
For nature prevents all contacts and stops up the channels.
As a consequence feeling is withdrawn to the depths
And since there is nothing left to sustain the organism
The body grows weak and all the limbs become limp;
The arms and eyelids droop, and even if you are lying down,
The knees will collapse and your legs lose all their strength.

And then sleep follows food, which works just like air
As soon as it is diffused through all the veins.
The drowsiness is much heavier if you are
Full up or weary, because when you are many elements
Fall in disorder bruised by so much exertion.
For the same reason the part of the soul which goes deep
Goes deeper and that which is scattered abroad goes further;
There is more division and dispersal inside you.

Whatever have been our habitual occupations,
Whatever the things on which we have spent most time
And whatever we have most exerted our minds on
— These are the things we usually see in dreams.
The lawyer finds himself pleading or drafting documents;
The general is engulfed in imaginary battles;
The sailor has a bad time with the weather;
I am working on this, examining natural processes
And writing down the results in my native language.
Other pursuits and interests in like manner
Appear to us in the deception of dreams.

When people have spent day after day at the games
They go on seeing them after they are away from them;
For in their minds the ways are still left open
Through which the images of such things may come.
For many days the same objects present themselves
Before their eyes and, even awake, they seem
To see the dancers moving their supple limbs
And to hear the liquid music of stringed instruments.
They see the flocks of people and still admire
The splendour and variegation of the scenery.
Such is the power of things which take our attention
And give us pleasure, and things we are always engaged on;
It is so not only with men but with all living creatures.

And often hunting dogs, although sound asleep,
Will suddenly throw out their legs and utter cries,
Sniffing about as if they were on the scent
And really following the track of some wild animal.
They may when they wake up still follow the image
Of the stags they imagine they see, until it fades
And they once more become their reasonable selves.

The same with the little pet dogs about the house:
They will shake themselves and suddenly stand up
As if they were seeing new faces in the room.
The fiercer the breed of animal, the more he exhibits
Fury in his dreams, his nature requires it.

But various kinds of birds take flight and the noise of their
                                                              wings
Breaks in the night-time on the sacred groves
If once in their dreams they think they see the hawk
Offering them violence and pursuing their flight.

What powerful movements the human mind may have:
Often in sleep the same things harry us still.
Men throw down kings; themselves are taken in battle;
They raise a shout as if their throats were cut.
Many will struggle, emitting horrible groans
And just as if a panther or lion had bitten them
Fill the place with the loudest possible cries.
Many will talk in sleep of important affairs;

It is not unknown for a man to speak of his crimes;
Many encounter death: and from high mountains
Have the impression of falling to sea-level;
They are terrified, and when they awake their minds
Are still so caught they hardly know what they are doing.
A man may feel thirsty and stop at the bank of a river
Or at a spring and offer to drink the lot.
Children often, when they are fast asleep,
Think they are on their pots or in the lavatory
And lift up their clothes and let out a whole bladderful,
Making a mess on a fine Babylonian carpet.

The adolescent, boiling for the first time
With seed inside him, ripened that very day,
Is met by images from some body or other
Suggesting a lovely face and a beautiful colour.
They rouse the parts which are swollen already with seed
Until, as if the whole thing was really happening,
He pours out a river which spills all over his tunic.

The seed is excited in us as I have explained,
As soon as our first maturity gives us the strength.
Different things are excited by different causes;
It needs a human creature to call up the seed.
As soon as it has been elicited from its recesses,
It is drained away from every part of the body
And, collecting in the appropriate nerve centres,
It stirs up the genital organs without delay.
Provoked by the seed, these places swell; and the impulse
Is to eject it towards the ominous object;
So the whole mind seeks the body which is causing the
damage.
Men usually fall on the side on which they are wounded;
The blood flows in the direction the blow comes from,
And straight at the enemy if he stands in the way.

It is the same with a man wounded by Venus' arrows,
Whether they come at him from a girlish boy
Or from a woman whose whole body hurls love at him;
He runs at the person who shot him and wants to copulate
And to plant in that body the fluid from his own body;
His dumb desire suggests it will give him pleasure.

That is Venus for you, it is that which we call Love;
That is the source of the sweetness which Venus pours
Drop by drop in our hearts: and then we are worried.
If what you want isn't there, there are always images
Of her, and her sweet name will ring in your ears.

Keep off imagination and frighten away
Whatever encourages love; turn your mind elsewhere,
Get rid of the fluid in any body you can
Instead of keeping it for a single person
Which is bound to lead to trouble and end in grief.
If you have an ulcer there is no point in feeding it,
The madness gets worse every day and the burden intolerable
If you do not confuse the first wound with several others
And wander and lose yourself in the general Venus:
Unless you can turn your mind to another subject.

No need to do without sex if you keep off love;
You simply have it without the disadvantages.
For surely those who are perfectly well have more pleasure
Than the afflicted: even in the moment of triumph
Lovers drift in all kinds of doubts and confusions,
Not knowing whether to start with the eye or the hands.
They squash the body they sought until it squeals
And often their teeth make a gash on the lips
In the course of affixing a kiss, which is hardly pure pleasure.
They are indeed rather provoked to injure the object,
Whatever it is, which causes this onset of lunacy.
But Venus mitigates pains such as these for the lover
And a gentle admixture of pleasure will soften the bite.

For the hope is always that the body which causes this
                                                   ardour
Will prove the best instrument for quenching the flame,
Which is quite contrary to the order of nature.
This is the one case in which the more we have
The more we burn with furious desire for more.
Food and drink are taken into the body,
They fill up certain spaces and that is that,
The craving for solitude and liquids is easily satisfied
But with human faces and beautiful complexions
There is nothing to take in and enjoy but a pack of images,

A wretched hope which the wind can blow away:
Just as when a thirsty man tries to drink in a dream
He cannot get a drop which will really slake his limbs,
He goes after imaginary liquid and labours in vain
And is thirsty even while drinking a raging river.
So in love Venus plays with her lovers in images;
They cannot be satisfied by looking at bodies
Nor can they scrape off bits of delicious limbs
But think they might and roam all over the body.

When with limbs together they enjoy the flower of their age
And the body has a premonition of pleasure,
With Venus ready to sow the feminine fields,
They catch at each other greedily, exchanging spittle,
And sigh in pressing each other's mouth with their teeth.
It is no good; they cannot get anything off;
They cannot get into the body with the whole body.
They seem to want to, however, and make immense efforts
To the point that they stick in the embraces of Venus
Until their limbs melt with the force of the pleasure.
When the desire in their sinews has made its eruption
There is a little pause in the violence of their ardour:
Then the lunacy breaks out again and the frenzy comes back
When they ask what it is they should like to obtain for
                                                    themselves
And cannot find any device which will make them feel
                                                    better,
So not knowing they pine away with a blind disease.

Besides, they use up their strength by overdoing it;
Not only that, they live at the whim of another.
Their money turns into Babylonian embroideries;
They neglect their business and their good name becomes
                                                    shaky;
There are perfumes; her feet must be shod in beautiful
                                                    slippers;
Enormous emeralds gleam on her, set in gold,
Yet the sea-coloured gown will wear out quickly enough
With all the amorous sweat that it has to mop up.
The patrimony turns into ribbons and headgear,
Dresses which come all the way from Alinda or Cos.
It all goes in dinners with clothes and expensive food,

Shows, lots of drink, and bath-salts and head-bands and
garlands.
Quite useless, for out of the source of so many attractions
Something bitter comes up, and the flowers are a pain.
Either the mind will reflect and become remorseful
At so much waste of time in pursuit of debauchery
Or else the girl lets drop some ambiguous expression
Which sticks in the heart and burns away like a fire,
Or possibly turns her eyes in the wrong direction
And lets fall the trace of a smile at somebody else.

These evils are found in the most prosperous love:
As to the ills of those who simply get nowehere
You can close your eyes and imagine how many they are:
They are innumerable: so better watch out
And take good care, as I said, that you don't get caught.
To avoid falling into an amorous entanglement
Is not so hard as to get out once you are in
For the knots Venus makes are very hard to untie.

But even if you are caught in the entanglement
You can avoid the worst if you don't stand in your own way
By blinding yourself to the faults of mind and body
There are in the person you are so keen to follow.
Yet this is exactly what men generally do;
They attribute qualities which are simply not there.
We often see mis-shapen, disgusting women
Regarded as charming, indeed, you might say worshipped.
Men will mutually give ironic advice
About horrible passions they notice in one another
Without the least regard to their own misfortunes.
A dark girl looks like honey; an unwashed one is natural;
The cat-eyed bitch is a goddess; the stringy one is a sylph;
The undersized, undergrown one a minute gem;
The overgrown monster has an extraordinary dignity;
The girl with a stammer has a bit of a lisp;
The dumb girl is just diffident; while the screaming,
Big-mouthed harpy is bubbling over with life;
A girl is slim when she is at death's door,
She is so thin; or sensitive, when she's consumptive;
If she has a mountainous bosom she is jolly;
If her nose is flat she's puckish; thick lips give a lovely kiss:
Really one can't go on with the recitation.

134

Even supposing the girl you love is beautiful
And her body has every kind of amorous attraction:
Still, there are others, and you did without her before;
And she does all the things the most unpleasant ones do
And chokes herself with the horrible smells she gives off
While her maids run away or snigger behind her back.

The tearful lover, shut out, will cover the entrance
With flowers and even garlands, while the splendid doorposts
He plasters with oil of marjoram, adding his kisses.
Yet if he were let in one whiff from the boudoir
Would make him think of excuses for getting away
And his long-thought-out complaint would be forgotten;
He would curse the stupidity which made him think of her
As somebody who wasn't actually mortal.
Our Venuses know all this and go to great pains
To keep such matters hidden behind the scenes:
It is hardly worth it; a little reflection will tell us
Just what is happening and why the servants are giggling.
If the girl is sensible and not full of pretences,
Be sensible too and allow her human functions.

The woman may sometimes be quite genuine
In embraces body to body with a man,
With a sucking of lips and a slobbering of kisses
She often acts in good faith and wants to share
The pleasure and begs the man to go on to the end.
It is just the same with birds, cattle and wild animals
To say nothing of sheep and mares, they would not put up
                                                     with the male
If, with the female on heat, there was no enthusiasm
For taking the leaping animal on her back.
And don't you see couples who are the evident victims
Of mutual pleasure, though they find their chains a torture?
There are often dogs in the street who want to separate
And pull in opposite ways with all their might
But stick none the less because Venus is too strong for them?
They wouldn't do it, if both didn't feel the pleasure
Which brought them into the trap and holds them prisoner;
So once again, that shows that the feeling is mutual.

In the mixing of seed, when the woman turns out the winner
And suddenly snatches what the man has to offer

135

The children are made after the woman's pattern
And so the other way round; and there are children
With a bit of both who take after both parents,
With their father's body and their mother's blood.
That happens when the ardour has been mutual
And elements from both bodies are well mixed up
And neither one nor the other had the better of it.
It also happens that children resemble their grandparents
Or even reproduce the shape of great-grandparents;
This is because the parents often conceal
In their bodies a great variety of elements
Handed down for generations from ancient stock.
So the chances of Venus produce all kinds of people
And bring back ancestors' faces and voices and hair
Which are just as much the products of certain seeds
As features and build of body or shape of limbs.
And the female is just as much from the father's seed
As the male will come out of the mother's body.
The child is always the fruit of a double seed
And the parent to which it has the most resemblance
Is the one it has most of: which may be observed
Equally in the male and female offspring.

There is no question of the power of the gods
Ever stopping anyone from being a father
Or making him pass his life in a sterile love
Though people say so and drench the altars with blood
And mournfully burn up a pile of sacrifices
Imploring seed which will give them gravid wives.
They are wasting their time with gods and oracles
For, if they are sterile, it is for one of two reasons:
Either the seed is too fluid or else too thick.
If it's too thin, it will not stick where it should
But flows back at once before its work is done;
Too thick, it comes out more solid than is suitable
And either does not penetrate far enough up,
Or cannot get at the right places or, having got in,
Is ill adapted to mix with the woman's seed.

The couplings of Venus offer a great variety:
Some men fertilize some women better than others
And women vary in what they need for pregnancy.

Many women who have been sterile in several marriages
Afterwards find a man who can make them pregnant
And they after all have the pleasure of having children:
And men whom fertile wives have left without children
Have in the end found somebody who is suitable
And so surrounded their old age with children.
So much importance attaches to the seeds
Being suitable to mix and fertilize,
Thick with fluid, and fluid with the thick.

Diet is of importance in this matter.
By some foods the seed is thickened in the body;
By others it is thinned out and wasted away.
The manner in which the pleasure is actually taken
Is of very great importance: the fashion of animals,
The manner in which the female quadruped takes it
Generally seems the best for securing conception.
The seed can get to its objective best
If wives put their breasts down and behinds in the air.
No need for wives to engage in lascivious movements:
The woman thereby is hindering conception.
If she wriggles her buttocks in pursuit of pleasure
And stimulates oceans by presenting a boneless front
She throws the furrow out from the right area
And stops the plough and the spurt of seed going home.
That is the reason prostitutes move that way,
Because they do not want to be pregnant too often
And want their men to have a well-devised pleasure:
Nothing of that sort seems necessary for wives.

Yet sometimes without the intervention of Venus
A rather sub-average woman may come to be loved.
She manages by herself and by what she does,
By compliant ways and keeping her body clean
To get a man used to sharing her existence.
For the rest, what you get used to you tend to love;
However light the blows, if they are repeated
They will end by bringing down whatever it is.
It has long been a matter of ordinary observation
That constant dripping wears away the stone.

BOOK V

Further praises of Epicurus, whose performance is preferred to that of several of the gods, as superstition presents them. Something more is said of the nature of the real gods, who are made of a substance so delicate that our senses cannot perceive them nor they touch anything that we can touch. The poet proceeds to an account of the beginning and end of our world, which is one of many; gives some astronomical explanations, and concludes with an account of the beginnings of civilization.

Who is skilful enough to produce an adequate poem
About the magnificent world and these discoveries about it?
Does anyone so use language that he can praise appropriately
The man who made these discoveries and left them for us?
I think the subject beyond an ordinary mortal,
For to put things in the way so superb a subject
Demands, Memmius, a person no less than that deity
Who first discovered the explanation of life
Which is now called Intelligence, and who had the ability
To rescue life from all its storms and darkness
And put it down in a calm and brilliant light.

Compare what he did with what the other gods did.
Ceres brought corn and Bacchus started the notion
Of making the most of the juice that comes from the vine.
Yet neither of these two gifts is indispensable
And travellers say some countries still do without them.
But you cannot live well unless your heart is unclouded.
Reason enough to consider that man as a deity
From whom we get these delightful consolations
Which soothe the mind and make life tolerable.

Or perhaps after all you have a preference for Hercules;
If you do let me tell you you are completely wrong.
Should we really worry now about the gaping
Jaws of the lion, or that boar in Arcady?
Or about that bull in Crete, or that plague in Lerna,
The hydra whose head was protected by poisonous snakes?
What about the triplet body of Geryon?

Or Diomede's horses breathing fire from their nostrils
In Thrace, along the Bistonian border and Ismara?
Do they matter all that much? Do we fear those harpies
With their raucous cries and their claws on Lake
                                    Stymphalus?
And the snake which had to look after the golden apples
Of the Hesperides, he certainly looked fierce
And had to wrap his enormous length round the tree;
What harm could he do on his remote Atlantic shore
Where we don't go and the savages don't dare to?
The same with all those monsters that were got rid of,
If they hadn't been killed, would they do much harm alive?
None at all, I think: for there are enough wild beasts
Even now; there is plenty to be afraid of
In woods, upon great mountains and in deep forests
But none the less we can generally avoid them.

But unless the heart is cleansed, what struggles we face,
What dangers, and hardly know how it comes about!
How bitterly are we torn if we let lust coax us,
What cares we have and then, what fears as well!
Or how much pride and filthiness and petulance
And what disasters! What self-indulgence and laziness!
The man who gets the better of all this
By words and without weapons, will not such a one
Deserve to be reckoned among the deities?
The more if he has himself given explanations
About the immortal gods and revelations
About the order of nature in its entirety.

Following his footsteps I too attempt to find reasons
And in my writings show how all is created
Within a system from which nothing can escape;
And that there are laws of time which must be obeyed.
And first, the soul itself is subject to them;
Formed of a body which itself was born
It cannot last intact throughout all ages;
It is only images cheat our minds in dreams
When we think we see someone whom life has abandoned.
For the rest, the general plan of my work now brings me
To show the mortality of the world itself,
That it too has a body which had a beginning.

I hope to show from what assembled material
The earth, sky, sea, stars, sun all came together
And the globe of the moon; what kinds of living creatures
Sprang out of the earth and what kinds never existed;
How the human race with different ways of talking
Began to converse by giving names to things;
And how it was that the fear of the gods found an entrance
Into men's minds, and now guards all over the world
Shrines, lakes, groves and altars and statues of gods.

Besides, I will deal with the course of sun and moon
And by what forces they are naturally steered
Lest you make the mistake of thinking their own free will
Sends them about the sky in sacred procession
Compliantly ripening corn and controlling destinies
Or imagine that they move by the will of the gods.
Even those who have taken the point that the gods are
                                                 indifferent
Sometimes wonder how the whole affair is managed
And are especially concerned about things overhead
Which they see rolling around so high in the heavens.
Once more they revert to the ancient superstitions
And take back those terrible masters they think all-powerful,
Not knowing that there are some things which can happen
And some which cannot, that every power is limited
By the system itself, and that everything has an end.

Not to spend any longer on this prospectus,
Memmius, first consider sea, earth and sky.
A threefold nature in which are three different materials,
Three different kinds of thing, or three different textures
— One day will see them all go, after so many years
And the whole mechanical giant will fall to pieces.
It does not escape me that this news will astonish you;
You will hardly credit that heaven and earth will vanish
And I shall find it hard to find words to persuade you:
It's like that when one puts forward something unfamiliar
And cannot put it to the test before people's eyes
Or let them handle it, which is much the best way
To convince anybody of anything.
Still, I will try; the event will prove what I say
Perhaps, and very shortly you may see

Tremendous earthquakes and everything falling to pieces.
Let us hope that the chances which govern things will
                                        avert this
And you will accept the reasoning without the persuasion
Of the universe coming to bits with a horrible crash.

But before I begin to expose the decrees of fate
More scrupulously and also with greater certainty
Than the Pythian priestess from the tripod and laurel of
                                        Phoebus,
I will go into this consoling matter quite thoroughly,
So that you don't superstitiously imagine
That earth and sun and sky, sea, stars and moon
Are divine material and ought to be everlasting;
Or take the view that, just like the giants and Titans
Anyone ought to be subject to criminal punishments
Who so to speak reasons away the walls of the world
And looks as if he wanted to put out the sun
And brand the everlasting with common speech.

These things in fact are far from any divinity
And certainly not to be counted among the gods;
They seem rather to be outstanding examples
Of the sort of thing which has neither life nor feeling.
It is not as if there were reason to think that mind
Can equally well exist in any body.
Trees cannot grow in the sky, and in the salt sea
You will find no clouds, and fish do not live in fields,
There is no blood in wood and there is no sap in rocks;
Everything grows and lives in fixed conditions:
It is the nature of mind that it cannot arise
Except in the body and close to the sinews and blood.
You might rather expect, I suppose, to find the intellect
In the head or shoulders or possibly in the heels
If it could pop up anywhere;
At least that would still be within the human container.
But as it seems that even within the body .
There is a fixed location where soul and mind can grow
There can be no reason whatever for asserting
They could hold their own outside any animal body,
In the crumbling soil or in the fire of the sun,
In water, or in the highest ethereal regions.

No question therefore of these things being divine
Since it is clear that they are not even alive.

It is moreover impossible that you should credit
That the gods can live in any part of the world.
Their nature is delicate and far from anything
Our senses perceive; it can hardly be seen by our minds.
And since it has always eluded the touch of our fingers
It must find intangible anything we can touch
For what cannot touch can certainly not be touched.
Therefore the gods must live in quite different conditions
From us, in mansions as delicate as themselves:
A point I will return to and deal with more fully.

To say that it was for the sake of men that the gods
Established this marvellous world and that on that account
We are in duty bound to praise their work
And even to believe that it will last for ever;
That it is blasphemy, in the face of their venerable wisdom
Which made all this for our eternal benefit
Ever to question what goes on in their residences,
To talk disrespectfully and turn things upside-down
— To go on like this is, I assure you, Memmius,
Absolute rubbish. These immortal and blessed beings
Could be none the better for any thanks we could give them:
Why should they therefore do anything for us?
What could have happened to make them want to change
Their way of life which had gone on smoothly so long?
Surely to get any pleasure out of novelties
Implies something wrong with what you have already?
But a being who has never known pain and has passed the
                                                time beautifully,
Whatever could make him itch for something new?
Or are we to think life was passed in shadows and sorrows
Till things were brightened up by a new generation?
Would it have hurt us not to have been created?
Admittedly once you are born you want to stay
But then there is pleasure to persuade you to keep alive.
But for one who has never tasted the Venus of living
What drawback could there be in not being born?

And where would the gods have found a model to work from
Or first got the notion of what man should be like?

How could they see in their minds what they wanted to
make?
How could they have known the properties of the elements
And the likely results of various combinations
If nature did not provide them with examples?
So many elements in so many ways
In collision with each other for infinite time
And always kept in motion by their weight
Attempted all possible ways of coming together
And every creation which could be so produced:
No wonder they have found the arrangement they have
And entered on the courses which gave us the universe
Which now persists by a constant self-renewal!

If I knew nothing of the nature of elements
Yet, given the behaviour of celestial bodies
And from other observations, I would conclude
That nature was not a divine invention
Intended for us: there is so much that is wrong with it.

In the first place, of all that the immense skies roll over,
There are the mountains and woods which ravenous beasts
Have taken possession of; there are rocks, vast marshes,
And the sea which keeps the various shores apart.
Two thirds are rendered useless to men by either
Blazing heat or else intolerable cold.
What is left for agriculture would be overrun
By thorns and the like if we did not take it in hand
In order to keep alive and, groaning in labour,
Turn up the earth all the time with hoe and plough.
If we did not turn the fertile soil with ploughshares
And work at it until the crops came up
They would not emerge into the air on their own.
And yet so often the product of all this labour,
When at last the leaves appear and everything flowers,
Is either burnt up by excessive heat
Or else is ended by the rains and frost
Or blown about by violent gales of wind.
What of all those terrifying breeds of wild animals
Which are dangerous to man on land or sea?
Why does nature encourage them? And why at all seasons
Are there so many sick? And why do so many die young?

143

The child is like a sailor cast up by the sea,
Lying naked on the shore, unable to speak,
Helpless, when first it comes to the light of day,
Shed from the womb through all the pains of labour,
And fills the place with cries as well it might,
Having a life of so many ills before it.
Yet flocks and herds, to say nothing of wild beasts,
Don't need a rattle or anything of that kind
Nor even a nurse to feed them with baby-talk:
Nor do they need sets of clothes for summer and winter.
One may add that they don't need weapons or high walls
To keep them safe, they find themselves perfectly happy
Walking around in a world which produces plenty.

To continue: since the bodies of earth and water,
The light breath of the air and the burning heat,
Out of which the whole of the universe is constructed,
Are none of them made of everlasting material
We must conclude that the whole world is mortal.
For everything of which the parts are clearly
Made of materials and shapes which do not last
Is, we can see for ourselves, unmistakably mortal
And has a beginning. So with the main parts of the world,
They are seen to be destroyed and grow again:
And no one knows that heaven and earth themselves
Have had a beginning and will have a disastrous end.

You are not to suppose that I have jumped to conclusions
Because I have said that earth and fire are mortal
And that I did not doubt water and air would perish
And be regenerated and grow again.
You will have observed that some part of the earth
Burnt by the sun or worn by passers' feet
Goes off in a cloud of dust which mounts in the air
And is carried and scattered by the powerful winds:
And that part of the soil is reduced to mud by the rain
And that rivers are always nibbling at their banks.
Moreover, whatever comes from the earth goes back to it,
Giving back just what it took, for as the earth is the mother
Of everything, so it is the common grave;
And so it is exhausted and replenished.

Then water: the sea and rivers and springs have plenty,
It is always replenished, the liquid is always flowing.
No need to labour the point: there is water everywhere
To prove it. Yet all the time just a little
Is taken off the surface, so it does not build up;
The powerful winds seep over and diminish it
Slightly: some of it is unravelled by the sun,
And some trickles away into the ground.
The impurities are strained off and the moisture itself
Trickles back and finds its way to the spring;
From there it flows overland, sweet once again,
Wherever any depression makes a way for it.

And what of air? The whole mass of it changes
By innumerable variations from hour to hour.
Something is always flowing from things, the losses
Are carried into the ocean of the air:
If nothing flowed back to replenish the substance of things
Before now everything would have been dissolved:
Air is regenerated all the time from things
And things in turn from air: for there is perpetual flux.

Likewise the fountain of light, the ethereal sun,
Constantly waters the sky with its latest brightness
So that light is always being replaced by light.
For every brilliant ray is lost at once
As soon as it falls. This fact is demonstrated
By the fact that when clouds pass below the sun
There is so to speak a break in the rays of light
And at once their lower end will disappear,
A shadow falls on the ground as the clouds drift by.
From this you see that things always need new light
And that once emitted a ray will always perish
So that nothing could be seen by the light of the sun
If the fountainhead itself did not supply it.

The lights we have at night, the hanging lantern,
And torches which with their brilliant horns of light
Send up a billowing mass of oily smoke,
Are hurrying all the time as they blaze away
To supply new light and tremble in every flame,
Pressing on so that there is never a break in the light:

So rapidly does one flame follow another
That the extinction of one is lost in a new flame starting.
One must conclude that sun and moon and stars
Throw off their light too by repeated emissions;
There is no reason to think them indestructible.

Do you not see even stone itself give way in time?
Do not great towers fall and rocks decay?
And what about the statues of the gods?
Divinity seems able to do little for them
And nothing at all against the course of nature.
It is the same with monuments put up to men,
They all fall down when they reach a good old age;
And are not chunks of rock torn from high mountains,
Unable to withstand the assaults of even
Limited time? For surely they wouldn't fall suddenly
If they could hold out to eternity
Unshaken by all the battery of age.

Look at what holds the earth in its embrace,
Round about and above us: if in fact, as people say,
It generates all things and finally takes them back
It must itself be subject to birth and death
For whatever increases and nourishes other bodies
Must be diminished, and recover when things come back to it.

Besides, if heaven and earth had no beginning
But were always there from all eternity
How does it happen the poets had nothing to say
Before the Theban war and the last rites of Troy?
Where have the deeds of all those heroes gone
Leaving no monuments for their remembrance?
The truth I think lies in the relative novelty
Of the universe; it has only just begun.
Why else should some arts still lack their final polish
And still be developing? For example, navigation
Is being improved; and music is still quite new.
Another recent discovery is the system
I am now explaining, and I am the first to be able
To put the subject plainly in our own language.

Or perhaps you believe it has all existed before
But that past generations have been somehow burnt up,

That cities were destroyed by gigantic earthquakes
Or that rains fell till the rivers all overflowed
And tore through the country and destroyed the towns:
If you do, you are all the more obliged to believe
That heaven and earth will also pass away.
For if things have been subjected to such great ills
And so many dangers, they might have been a bit worse
And ruined everything in one grand disaster.
It is in this way we understand we are mortal
For we see one another suffering from various diseases
Which have already carried other people away.

To proceed: anything which is eternal must be
Either composed of a solid body and so
Able to repel blows, and impenetrable so that
It will not split into parts; as, for example
The elements of matter, as I have demonstrated:
Or able to last through infinite time because
It is immune from blows as emptiness is
Which cannot be touched, so that there is no impact:
Or else because there is no space around it
Into which it could retreat on breaking up;
As is true of the totality of things
— There is nothing beyond it into which things can spring
apart
Or where there could be anything like a collision.
But I have shown that the world is in fact not solid;
Its nature is such that there are empty spaces in everything.
Nor is it like the void. And there is no lack of matter
Which could collect far out in infinite space
And arrive in a whirlwind to break everything up
Or bring some other disaster upon the world.
And there is no lack of space in the outer depths
Into which the walls of the world could fall to pieces
Or where they could collide and perish in that way.
So the gates of death are not closed either for the heavens,
For the sun or the earth or for the depths of the sea;
There is an immense gulf waiting to devour them
— Which carries the implication that they had a beginning,
For nothing of which the body is perishable
Could possibly have withstood for infinite time
The forces which are inseparable from time.

And since the constituents of the world are at war
With one another and never give any quarter,
Must you not suppose that sooner or later the conflict
Will have an end? Perhaps the sun and the other heats
Will have drunk up all the moisture and so got their way,
As they are always trying to do, though so far without
                                                    success;
The rivers provide so much water and threaten themselves
To flood the whole world by emptying the sea upon it.
They don't succeed either, for the winds sweep the surface
And keep it down, and the sun takes some of it off,
And together they hope to be able to dry up everything
Before the water can do what it looks like doing.
There is this undecided battle between things
Which strive to have the mastery of the world
As, at one time, fire is said to have dominated
And at another, the earth was under a flood.
Fire won and burnt part of the world to ashes
The day the horses of the sun all bolted
Dragging Phaeton across both sky and land.
But the omnipotent Father, in a rage,
Struck him with a sudden thunderbolt
Free of the horses, and the sun, which caught him
As he fell down from the burning lamp of the world,
Pulled the horses together and got them trembling in hand
Then put them back on their accustomed track
— At any rate, according to the Greek poets,
Which as usual is a long way from the truth.
Fire can predominate, when the material
Which constitutes it throngs in from the infinite:
Then its grip weakens and something else takes control
Or everything is burnt up in the blazing air.
Water once nearly had a similar victory,
So it is said, when it poured through many cities;
Then, when it receded, stopped by some force or other
Which happened to come rolling in from the infinite
The rain gave over and the rivers abated.

Now I will explain how the concourse of matter
Formed the foundation of earth, sky and sea
And ordered the motion of the sun and moon.
It certainly wasn't by conscious deliberation

The elements chose their places; they showed no intelligence;
Nor did they negotiate their respective movements:
It is simply that elements have been impelled
In innumerable ways and for an infinite time
And carried onwards as usual by their own weight,
Have come together in all ways and tried everything
Which can be engendered by their congresses,
And so it has happened that after ages of random wandering,
When every possible movement had been attempted,
That in the end they suddenly came together
In such a way as to bring about the beginnings
Of earth, sea, sky and of the human race.

At that time the disc of the sun was not to be seen,
No light from that, no stars in the firmament,
No sea, no sky, no sign of the earth or air
Nor indeed of anything like the things we know,
But a strange sort of weather with great bulks gathering
Of every kind of element, utter confusion
Of distances, ways, connections, weights and shocks,
Collisions and movements, everything warring with
           everything
Because forms were without resemblances to each other
And there was no possibility of maintaining unions
And ill-suited shapes were unable to come together.
Then part began to separate and like met with like,
The world was divided off and its limbs took shape;
The great parts that we know found their dispositions,
That is, high heaven was divided from the earth,
The sea took itself apart with its separate waters
And the fires of the outer atmosphere went away and
           burned.

What happened was that the elements of the earth
First came together, being heavier and more entangled
And took possession of the lower and central regions,
Then squeezed out the elements which were to compose
Sea, stars, sun, moon and the great walls of the world,
All of which were made of lighter and rounder elements,
Very much smaller than those which compose the earth.
So ether broke through the various pores of the earth,
Being light, and took with it a host of fires:

It was rather like what we have often seen
When in the morning the sun's rays redden the dewdrops
Hanging upon the grass, and the mist is exhaled
From lakes and from the inexhaustible rivers
And soon it looks as if all the earth is steaming:
All of which comes together again high up
And is woven into a heavy covering of cloud.
In the same way when the light and expansive ether
Spread out on all sides and encompassed the world
Diffusing itself in all directions everywhere
Till it held everything in its smooth embrace.

After this the beginnings of sun and moon
Which turn in the air between the earth and the ether:
Neither earth nor the ether has assimilated them.
They were neither heavy enough to sink to the one
Nor light enough to find their way out to the other.
So they stay between the two and, like living bodies,
They move and you may say form a part of the world.
It is just as we ourselves may be mainly still
While none the less some of our limbs are in motion.

When these things had been taken out, the earth
In the parts where now the vast seas lie with their blue
Sank and filled their depressions with salt floods.
And day by day, as the burning heat of the ether
And the rays of the sun beat on the land from all sides,
It shrank and was drawn together about its centre
And as it did the salt sweat poured from its body,
Increasing drop by drop the far-stretching sea;
The elements of sea and air flew up
To set into glittering spaces far from the earth.
The plains sank down, the mountains stood out more steeply
Because the rocks were unable to subside
So that all was not reduced to a uniform level.

That is how the earth became so compact and heavy
And all the slime sank to the lowest places
And settled there as a sort of sediment.
Then all the sea, then the air and lastly the burning ether,
All fluid bodies, were left as if decanted.
They are not all equally light; the ether, as lightest

And the most liquid, flows on top of the air,
Keeping its liquid body free of the gales
Below; and allows things below to be blasted
By hurricanes and troubled by wayward storms:
The fires of the ether glide on changelessly,
Carried by the stream, and how that stream may flow
You may learn from the Pontus, which flows with a
                                                changeless current,
For ever keeping the same gliding course.

I go on to explain the movements of the stars.
And first, if it is the whole of the sky which turns
The air must press with particular force on the poles
And hold them so that at those points there is no movement
While another current flows in the direction
The glittering stars follow in their rotation;
Or else the current flows underneath the world
As we see rivers turn a water-wheel.

On the other hand the whole sky may stay still
While the brilliant stars are somehow carried across:
Either because there are rapid currents of ether
Circulating as they look for a way out
And these carry the stars and determine their orbit;
Or else a current of air coming from outside
Accounts for their movements: or they glide by themselves
In search of food and go wherever they find it,
Feeding on elements of flame here and there in the sky.
It is not easy to establish with certitude
The cause of events in this world; my aim is rather
To show what is possible anywhere in the universe
In various worlds formed upon various plans
And to set out the several causes which might operate
Throughout the universe to move the stars.
Only one of these can operate in our sky
And I will not venture to say which it might be;
The advance of knowledge is inevitably gradual.

For the earth to rest as it does in the middle of our system
Its weight must gradually decrease to vanishing point
So that underneath it is of a different nature
And has been from its beginnings

One with the air in which it is embodied.
That is why it has no weight and can ride on air:
Rather as a man does not feel the weight of his limbs
And the head does not weigh on the neck, and we do not
feel
The whole weight of our bodies upon our feet
While any burden placed on us from outside
We feel at once, though the weight may be much less:
Which shows how the circumstances make a difference.
The earth does not therefore rest upon alien material
But is cushioned by something which has the nature of air
And was conceived with it from the beginning of the world,
A part of the system as our limbs are part of us.

When the earth is struck by a sudden clap of thunder
The whole of the atmosphere above it shakes
Which could not happen in this way if earth were not
Joined somehow or other to the air and sky.
They are, indeed, fixed by their common roots
And have been together since the beginning of time.
Do you not see how, for all the weight of the body,
The soul with its subtle nature can support it
Because they have always been together as one?
And what could lift the body when it leaps in the air
Except the strength of the soul which controls the limbs?
So you see how a subtle nature can be strong
When joined to a heavy body, and that is the case
With air and the earth and with ourselves and our soul.

The disc of the sun must be the same size, more or less
As it seems to our senses, and just about as hot,
For however far it may transmit its heat
The distances take nothing from the mass of flames
And it does not appear any smaller than it is.
The heat of the sun and the light which it pours out
Arrive at our organs of sense and fall on the earth,
So its form and size must be as they appear
Without indeed addition or subtraction.

Whether the moon as it is carried on its way
Shines with a borrowed light or with its own,
Whatever substance it's made of it does not appear

To be any bigger than what we see with our eyes,
For anything we see a long way away
Through a mass of air, grows hazy to us before
It grows any smaller: and since with the moon
We see a clear outline and a definite figure
It must as it stands on high be seen by us
As exactly of the size which it actually is.

Now as to the rest of the lights we see in the sky.
We know that with lights and fires we see on earth
As long as the flickering of their flames is visible
Their size appears to be very little changed
One way or another, whatever may be the distance.
The same with the stars: we must see them as they are,
A little larger or smaller, but that is all.

There is no cause for astonishment that the sun,
Little as it is, can send forth so much light
As to flood both land and sea and the whole sky
And pour over everything warm exhalations.
It is possible that a spring for the whole world
Flows from this spot and shoots out abundant light
Because it is here that the elements of heat
Converge from all sides and, collecting round about,
Gush out to warm the world from a single spring.
Haven't you seen how a little trickling stream,
Watering a meadow, in time can flood whole plains?
It is possible that the heat from the sun's fire,
Without being great, can master the whole air
If the intervening atmosphere is so constituted
That it can catch alight from the smallest heat:
It is the kind of thing we see sometimes
When corn or stubble flares from a single spark.
Or perhaps the sun we see as a glowing lamp
Has around it masses of invisible fire,
Something which does not give out any light
Yet carries heat and reinforces the sun's rays.

There is likewise no simple, self-evident explanation
Of the way the sun moves from its summer positions
To reach the midwinter turning-point in Capricorn
And turns again towards the tropic of Cancer;

Nor of why the moon seems to cross in only a month
The space which the sun will take a year to complete:
If there is a simple cause I have not found it.
It seems very likely that Democritus was right
In the opinion he expressed on the matter,
That the nearer constellations are to the earth
The less rapidly they are carried by the whirlwind above it.
The force and rapidity of the blast is diminished
As one gets nearer the earth, and so the sun
Is gradually left behind with the slower stars
Which like it are far below the other constellations.
The moon even more so: and the lower her path,
The further away it is from the top of the sky
And the nearer to earth, the less she can keep pace.
For the less the force of the gale which carries her
Below the sun, the more do all the stars
Catch up and pass her as they sweep around.
So she appears to come back to each star
More quickly, as the stars come back to her.

Another possibility is that two winds,
Blowing alternately across the sun's course,
Drive it first from its summer route until it reaches
Its winter turning-point in the freezing cold
Then back to the summer sky and the short nights.
Likewise one may think that the moon as well as those stars
Which make great revolutions in great years
Are driven in turn by alternate streams of air.
Have you not seen how clouds, some above the others,
Will pass one another from quite opposite directions?
Why should the same not happen with the stars
Carried in opposing directions in the ether?

When the night covers the whole of our lands with darkness
It is either because the sun, at the end of its course,
Worn out by the journey, has breathed its last fires,
Stamped out by all the air which has buffeted it:
Or else the force which has driven it across our sky
Carries it round the earth under our feet.

At a fixed time too there is pink at the distant edge
Of the sky, the morning is here and the light pours out;

Either because the sun comes back from below
And tries to scatter its rays before it climbs
Or because fires come together and many elements
Of heat flow into one place at that fixed hour
And make the sun afresh at that time every morning:
As it is said that on the summit of Ida
The scattered fires can be seen assembling at dawn
Till they form a single ball and we see a circle.

It is not a matter which ought to cause astonishment
That the elements of fire come so precisely
At the right time to make the sun's brilliance afresh.
We see many things which happen at certain times
In the order of nature. There is flowering at certain times
For trees and at certain times they shed their blossoms.
So too age causes the teeth to fall out when they do
And the body hair appears at adolescence
At the same time as the beard creeps down the cheeks.
Even lightning, snow, rain, clouds and winds break in
At more or less definite times in every year.
The causes which have brought them about are the same
As they ever were from the beginning of the world
And they come round again in a consequential order.

Likewise the days may lengthen and nights grow short
Or daylight lessen with the increase of darkness
Because the sun, above and below
The earth, moves in unequal segments of its ellipse
And so divides its course into unequal parts.
What it takes from one part it gives back to the other
So that anything lost in one way is gained in another,
Until it arrives at that point in the sky
At which the duration of day and night are equal.
For when the sun's course is half-way between the blasts
Of north and south winds, the termini of its journeys
Are at exactly equal distances from their beginnings
Because of the position of the whole zodiac
Through which the sun glides in the course of the year,
Lighting up both earth and sky with its light:
As is shown by the diagram in which astronomers
Have noted the position of all the constellations.

Or it may be the air is thicker in certain parts
So that the trembling fire is stuck below the earth
And cannot easily reach the point at which it rises;
That would cause the slowness of the long winter nights
Before a ray appears to bring the daylight;
Or it may be that at different times of the year
Fire flows together more slowly or more quickly
Which would cause the sun to rise at a certain point.

The moon may shine because struck by the rays of the sun
And turn her light increasingly towards us
The further she recedes from the ball of the sun
Until just opposite him she shines out full
And at her rising watches the sun go down:
Then slowly reversing her steps she must hide her light
In the same way, the nearer she slides to the sun,
Passing through the other half of the zodiac;
That is the theory of those who think that the moon
Is a ball which runs below the course of the sun;
Which seems to me a true hypothesis.
It may be, however, that the moon has her own light
And turns and shows the various shapes of her brightness.
There may be some other body which turns with the moon,
Obscuring her light in varying degrees as it moves,
A body which cannot be seen since it has no light.
It may be the moon is a globe which turns on its axis
And that half of it is steeped in a blazing light
So that when it turns we see it in various shapes
Until the part which is all aglow with fire
Is turned directly towards us as we look;
Then it turns gradually back and as it does carries
The brilliant part of the globe out of our sight:
That is the view taken by the Chaldeans
Who seek to refute the theories of the astronomers
As if one or other hypothesis must be absurd
Although one is just as credible as the other.

Or why should not a new moon be created
All the time, with a set succession of shapes,
Failing from day to day and then re-created,
Each giving way and another taking its place?
It is hard to prove that this is not what happens

156

When you see so many things created in series.
Spring comes, and Venus with her, and ahead of Venus
Her winged forerunner, the spring breeze, and Flora
Her mother strews the way with flowers
And fills the world with marvellous colours and scents.
The next in order is the scorching heat, and Ceres
Her dusty companion, and the yearly winds from the north.
Then autumn advances with Bacchus and the Bacchantes;
Then other winds and other weathers will follow,
The roaring southeaster, the south wind full of lightning.
The solstice brings the snows and the numbing cold
And winter follows next with chattering teeth.
It could well happen, therefore, that the moon
Is new-made at certain times and destroyed at others
Since so many other things are certainly seasonal.

There is reason to think that solar and lunar eclipses
Must be attributed to one of several causes.
Why must it be the moon which can intercept
The sun's light and block the view from the earth
By thrusting its blind form across the burning rays?
Why should it not equally well be thought
That some other body interposes itself,
One which is always in motion but gives no light?
Or why should it not be that the sun, at a certain time,
Is exhausted and loses its fire, to give light again
When it has passed, perhaps, through certain areas
Of such a nature that fires cannot burn in them?
And why should the earth be able to keep light from the
                                                    moon
And hold back the sun's rays while the moon is in shadow
Or partly so, during her monthly circuit,
If it is not possible for some other body
On the same timetable to slide below the moon
Or in front of the sun and so block off the light?
And if the moon is the source of its own light
Why should it not grow dim in certain areas
As it passes through, if they do not tolerate light?

Now that I have given a possible explanation
Of all that we see happen up there in the heavens,
Including the course of the sun and the moon

And what produces them, and of how it can happen
That sometimes their light is intercepted and lost,
Causing surprise on earth by producing darkness
As if there were an eye which sometimes shut
And opened again when the world is flooded with light;
Now I go back to the early days of the world
When the ground was soft and gave birth to new productions
Committing them to the care of the wayward winds.

At first there was vegetation and shining green
All over the hills and across the level places;
The flowering meadows glittered with bright green;
The different trees rose high in the air,
Competing and with nothing holding them back.
Like first feathers and hair and bristles appearing
On the naked bodies of quadrupeds and birds
The new earth shot out grass and shrubs at first
And then went on to produce the mortal animals,
Great numbers of them, starting in various ways.
The animals cannot have fallen from the sky
Nor those that live on land have come out of the sea.
No wonder therefore the earth is called our mother
Since every creature came out of the ground.
Many creatures still exist underneath;
It takes the rain and sun to bring them up:
The less cause for wonder, therefore, that more and larger
                                                     creatures
Were brought to birth when the earth and air were young.

First of all the winged creatures, every kind of bird,
Left the eggs, hatched out in the spring season;
As still in summer the cicadas cast their coats
To seek the food they need in order to live.
Then it was the earth first gave forth races of animals
For at that time the ground was wet and warm.
And so, wherever there was a suitable spot
Were breeding-places attached to the earth by roots
And the young came out when they were ready to come,
Getting away from the wet and seeking for air.
Nature turned towards them the pores of the earth
Out of which it forced from its veins a liquid like milk:
Just as now a woman who has a child is filled

With milk and the current of nutriment flows at her nipples.
Earth then fed the babies and heat clothed them
And the grass provided a soft, well-padded cradle.

In the early days of the world there were no hard frosts
Or excessive heats, and the wind did not blow violently.
Everything grew in unison and grew strongly.
So I say again, you can call the earth our mother,
She deserves the name, she created the human race
And at a determined time poured out all species
Of animals which wander joyfully on the great mountains
As well as the birds of the air in their various shapes.

But since all fecundity must have an end, she gave up
Like a woman who is past the time of childbearing.
Time changes the nature of the whole world;
Everything passes from one state to another
And nothing stays like itself: all things pass away;
Nature obliges everything to change about.
One thing crumbles and falls in the weakness of age;
Another grows in its place from a negligible start.
So time alters the whole nature of the world
And earth passes from one state to another:
She can no longer bear what she could, but she bears what
                                              before she could not.

At that time the earth created many monsters
Which came out with extraordinary faces and bodies,
The androgyne, neither one sex nor the other
But between the two: there were creatures without hands
                                              or feet;
Mutes without mouths, blind creatures with nothing to
                                              look with,
And some with arms and legs stuck to their bodies
So that they could not do anything or go anywhere,
Evade disaster or get what they needed for survival.
All such monsters were born without a future;
Their nature was such that they could not increase;
They never had a chance of reaching maturity;
They could not find food or make a sexual connection.
We know that many conditions must be satisfied
If a species is to last and reproduce itself:

159

First there must be food for it, and then a channel
Through which the genetic particles in the limbs
Can find a way out; and the female must fit the male;
There must be organs which can give mutual pleasure.

Many species will have died out at this period,
Not having the capacity to continue their race.
For wherever you see a creature which has survived
It is craft or strength or mobility that has saved it,
Affording protection from the very beginning.
There are many animals which have survived because
They were useful enough to us for us to protect them.
With lions and other beasts of like ferocity
It was strength which preserved them; with the fox it was
                                          craftiness;
With deer it was speed. But the light-sleeping, faithful dog
And all the various species of beasts of burden
As well as sheep (for their wool) and all sorts of cattle,
All these were consigned to men to look after, Memmius.
They were anxious to escape wild beasts and live in peace
And obtain plenty of food without any labour;
We gave them all that but the price was, they had to be
                                          useful.
However, the animals nature endowed with none of these
                                        qualities,
Who were neither able to live after their own manner
Nor to render us any service for which we would tolerate
Their living at our expense and being protected
— These it is clear would merely be prey for others,
As it were entangled in their unfortunate selves
Until nature brought their race to complete destruction.

But centaurs never existed; there could never be
So to speak a double nature in a single body
Or a double body composed of incongruous parts
With a consequent disparity in the faculties.
The stupidest person ought to be convinced of that.

In the first place, it is only a matter of three years
Before a horse is fully grown. Not so with a child!
At that age he may in sleep still grope for the nipple.
Later, when the horse finds his old body grown tired

And his strength is almost gone, the boy on the contrary
Is just at the point where the flower of his age begins
And the down begins to appear upon his cheeks.
So do not imagine that the seed of men and of horses
Together make a centaur, or that such a beast
Could survive in any case; nor that there are Scyllas
With half-aquatic bodies and a chain of mad dogs
About their middles; nor anything of that kind.
The parts of such creatures would not harmonize;
They grow up at different rates, and their whole
$\qquad$ development
Right to old age is subject to different laws.
Their sexual urges are different, as well as their habits
And the whole of their bodies seek different satisfactions;
For example you may have seen goats grow fat on hemlock
Which is to man among the deadliest of poisons.

Flame will burn the tawny bodies of lions
As well as the flesh of any other animal
And any blood which ever flowed in their veins.
How could there, therefore, be a triple creature,
Part lion, part dragon and in the middle chimaera,
Breathing out biting flames from its inside?

Anyone who imagines that when earth and sky were new
Animals of that kind could be engendered
Is simply over-impressed with the word 'new'
And will quickly be led to utter other absurdities,
Alleging perhaps that in those times rivers of gold
Flowed through the land, or that diamonds grew on trees;
Or that a man born then might be so huge
That he could easily stride across the sea
Or spin the whole sky round by using his hands.
The fact that there were many genetic elements present
At the time when the earth first poured out living creatures
Does not mean that she could then have produced
Hybrid animals made up of disparate parts.
The vegetation of various kinds which still
Springs from the ground, the corn, the trees and the like,
Is not all mixed together, the species are separate.
Each thing has developed its own particular rites
And keeps the characteristics that nature gave it.

The race of man at that time in the fields
Was harder, having come from the hard ground.
They were constructed inside of larger bones,
Stronger than ours, and their flesh was entirely sinuous.
It took more than heat or cold to exhaust such men;
They ate whatever offered and were not sick.
Through many repetitions of the sun's course
They followed a wandering life as wild beasts do.
They did not employ their energies at the plough
And did not know the use of iron in agriculture
Nor how to plant saplings, or lop boughs from old trees.
Whatever the sun and rain gave them they took
And were content with what earth grew on her own.
An oak-tree bearing acorns gave them enough
In the ordinary way, with the berries which you see still
On the arbutus in winter, red when they are ripe,
But larger and more numerous in those days.
The young earth bore a variety of coarse crops,
More than enough for the needs of its wretched inhabitants.

Rivers and springs called men to slake their thirst
As now from high mountains the course of descending
water
Summons wild beasts from far and wide with its noise.
As they wandered in the night they came upon
The wooded haunts of nymphs, out of which, they knew
Water would come splashing over the rocks,
The rocks dripping and covered with wet green moss,
And part of it bubbling out over the level.

They did not know what uses fire could be put to,
Nor how to dress themselves in wild beasts' skins.
They lived in groves and caves and in the forests
And sheltered their dirty bodies in the undergrowth
When buffeting winds and rain became too much.
They had no notion at all of the common good,
Understanding nothing of custom or of law.
The man who was lucky and found some prey went off
with it,
The only idea they had was: Each man for himself;
And Venus coupled their bodies in the forest;
What brought them together was either that both wanted it,

That the man was violent and his lust was threatening,
Or some such gift as acorns, berries and pears.

Trusting to the marvellous powers of their hands and feet
They would follow the tracks of wild beasts in the woods
And attack them with showers of stones, or club them
                                                    down;
They could get the better of most, but a few they fled
And like bristly swine they would throw themselves on the
                                                    ground
Naked, whenever the night came down upon them,
Covering themselves as best they could with leaves.
Yet there was no question of waiting for the day
Or wandering around in terror looking for it;
They waited silently and buried in sleep
Till the sun with its red beacon brought back the light.
Accustomed from childhood to night and day
Being produced in turn in constant succession,
It never occurred to them to be astonished,
Nor to fear that the night when it came might last for ever.
They were much more concerned about the savage beasts
Which would often make a sleep the end of everything:
Driven from the shelter of their rock or cave
By the arrival of a wild boar or a lion
At dead of night and in an access of terror
They would give up their pile of leaves to their savage guest.

There was not much more death about then than there is now
And little occasion to part with life with laments.
No doubt it happened more often that some wild beast
Got hold of someone and so made a lively dinner,
The hills and forests would be filled with moaning
As the man saw his flesh going into a living grave.
If anyone escaped with a piece bitten out of him
He would clutch his horrible wounds with trembling hands
And call for an end to it all with a strident voice
Until his writhings saw him out of the daylight
Without help and with no idea what help was wanted.
On the other hand there was then no dying in thousands
In a single day in a military formation;
Nor was there any danger of being shipwrecked.
The sea often raged of course but it brought about nothing

And had in the end to withdraw its empty threats;
Nor was there any question of a calm surface
Enticing anyone with its treacherous smiles.
The desperate business of going to sea was unknown.
In those days it was starvation which finished men off
And now the same result is produced by plenty.
Then people accidentally poisoned themselves;
Now with great skill they poison one another.

The next step was the use of huts and skins and fire,
And women became the property of one man.
So the chaste pleasures of a private Venus
Were first invented and couples had their own children.
It was then that the human race began to soften.
Fire had the effect of making bodies less able
To bear the cold under the open sky;
Venus reduced their strength, and children with
                                        endearments,
Easily broke down the stiff pride of their parents.
Then people first began to have friends and neighbours,
They did not seek to injure or treat with violence;
They gave a certain protection to women and children
And made it known in confused gestures and speech
That there ought to be some pity for those who are weak.
Of course they could not establish general peace
But a good proportion of people behaved in good faith;
If they hadn't, the human race would soon have died out
And the present would do without us and our breed.

Nature impelled men to make sounds with their tongues
And they found it useful to give names to things
Much for the reason that we see children now
Have recourse to gestures because they cannot speak
And point their fingers at things which appear before them.
Everyone tries to use the powers that are in him:
And calves will butt before they have grown their horns.
The young of the panther and of the lioness
Fight with their claws and feet and teeth before
They have really got any teeth or claws to fight with.
In the same way we see that birds of every kind
Begin to trust their wings before they can fly.

Therefore to think that somebody handed out names
To things and that this is how men first learned to speak
Is idiotic: for if one man could so designate
Objects, and make all the various sounds with his tongue
Why could not others do the same thing at the same time?

Besides, if others too had not made use
Of words among themselves, how could they have guessed
Words might be useful? And how could one man get the idea
In his mind in the first place and see what he wanted to do?
And one man could hardly force many to do as he fancied,
To see the point of learning the names of things.
It isn't easy to make the deaf understand
What one wants to teach them; those early men would not
                                        have stood for it
Nor seen any reason to put up with all that noise
Being drummed into ears which naturally understood none
                                        of it.

Lastly, what is there so strange about the fact
That the human race, with a powerful voice and tongue,
Should designate different impressions by different sounds?
Since even dumb cattle, to say nothing of wild beasts,
Are in the habit of uttering different cries
In fear or pain and when they are bursting with joy.
These are matters which you can learn by observation.

When in rage the great soft lips of Molassian dogs
Begin to curl back and show their naked teeth,
They threaten with a growl which is quite different
From the sound they make when they bark at the tops of
                                        their voices;
And when they are licking their young with a loving tongue
Or when they are tossing them, or pretending to bite them,
And make out they are going to swallow them,
It is again with a different sort of voice
From the one they use if they are left alone in a house
Or if they are trying to escape from a beating.

There seems to be a difference between the whinny
Of a young stallion among a crowd of mares
When he is ridden and spurred by the rage of love

And that when with nostrils dilated he snorts a war-cry
Or when his limbs all tremble and he whinnies.

Lastly, we see it with birds of various kinds;
Hawks and ospreys and gulls which seek their living
Among the salt waves, call in a different tone
When they are squabbling over a meal or struggling with
prey.
And some of them change their raucous song with the
weather,
As is the case with the ancient race of crows
And with flocks of rooks, when they are supposed to be
asking
For a downpour of rain and they are calling the wind.
Therefore, if different feelings can cause the animals,
Which are said to be dumb, to utter in different voices,
How much more proper it is to suppose that men
Should mark the distinction between things with different
sounds.

If I may anticipate a possible question,
It was lightning first brought fire down here for mortals
And that is the source of all the flames we have.
How many things do we see set ablaze by lightning
When a stroke from the sky has suddenly raised their
temperature.
And without this, when a branching tree rocks to and fro
In the wind, so that one branch rubs on that of another tree,
Sometimes the friction will produce a fire
And suddenly there will be a burst of flame
Which is caused by the rubbing together of the branches.
Men could have got fire from either of these sources.

Then the cooking of food: the softening of it by heat,
Was learned from the sun, which men saw soften many
things
As its rays poured down on them in the summer fields.
So from day to day they changed their food and their way
of living
By new ways of using fire, which the most inventive
And ingenious among them pointed out to the rest.

Kings began to found cities and construct fortresses
To serve as strong places and a refuge when necessary;
They divided the land and cattle and gave them out
To those who were beautiful, strong or showed intelligence.
Beauty and strength were, both of them, much esteemed;
Then wealth was discovered and soon after gold
Which quickly became more honoured than strength or
beauty.

For men, however strong or beautiful,
Generally follow the train of a richer man.

But if anyone were to conduct his life by reason
He would find great riches in living a peaceful life
And being contented; one is never short of a little
But men want always to be powerful and famous
So that their fortune rests on a solid foundation
And they can spend a placid life in opulence.
There isn't a hope of it; to attain great honours
You have to struggle along a dangerous way
And even when you reach the top there is envy
Which can strike you down like lightning into Tartarus.
For envy, like lightning, generally strikes at the top
Or any point which sticks out from the ordinary level.
So it is better to submit and live in quiet
Than to want to be the master of several kingdoms.
Let people wear themselves out, let them sweat blood,
Struggling up the narrow road of ambition;
Since they know no more than they hear from the mouths
of others
And go for what they have heard, not what they perceive;
That is how things are and have been and will be.

So the kings were killed and that was the end of thrones
In their pristine majesty, and of the pride of sceptres:
The crowned head, covered in blood, was kicked around
By the feet of the mob and had cause for dusty tears:
It is pleasant to trample on something that we have feared.
Power then went to the lowest dregs of the mob,
Everyone fancied that he should be the top man.
Then some men had the idea of setting up magistracies
And establishing codes so that people could live by law.
For the human race had grown tired of anarchy

With its hostilities and so more easily yielded
Of its own free will to live under legal restrictions;
The vengeance which individuals exacted in anger
Was worse than is now enjoined under regular laws
— One can understand why men were sick of anarchy.
After that fear of punishment spoiled the prizes.
Violence and wrong catch people in their own nets
And those who start such things are most often entangled.
It is not easy to pass a peaceful life
If you act in a way that disturbs the general peace.
Although you elude the gods and the human race
You still must wonder whether your secret will keep for
                                                    ever.
Are there not many people who talk in their sleep?
Or might not some word escape you in a delirium?
Crimes long concealed have come to light that way before.

Now what is the reason for the belief in the gods
Which has spread to all nations and filled their cities with
                                                    altars?
What has given support to all those sacred rites
So prominent everywhere on great occasions?
What is the source of that deep-seated terror
Which has raised sanctuaries all over the world
And has compelled men to celebrate holy days?
It is not so difficult to explain all this.

Even in those time mortals would see the gods
In imagination, even when awake,
And in their dreams they were all the more impressive.
They attributed feelings to them because they saw
Their limbs move and heard them speak fine words
Suitable for such powerful and good-looking beings.
They thought them immortal, because they were always
                                                    appearing
And yet somehow their form remained the same;
And because, after all, with all that strength they had,
One could hardly imagine anyone getting the better of them.
They thought them the most fortunate of beings
Because they could not be troubled by the idea of death
And because in their dreams they saw them do marvellous
                                                    things
Without showing even the faintest sign of fatigue.

Besides, they saw the order of the celestial system
And how the seasons came round without mistake;
They did not guess at all how all that could happen
So they took refuge in attributing it all to the gods
And supposed they did it by a nod of the head.

They assumed the sky was where the gods would live
Because that was where the sun and the moon had their
                                                        residences,
The moon, the day, the night and the solemn stars of night,
The meteors that wander by night, the flying flames,
Clouds, dew, rain, snow; the winds and lightning and hail;
The sudden rumblings and threatening murmurs of thunder.
O miserable human race, which attributes such acts
To the gods and then supposes them bitterly angry!
What troubles they made for themselves, what harm they
                                                        did us,
What tears we shall leave behind for our descendants!

It is not piety to be repeatedly seen
Turning a veiled head towards a piece of stone
And making sure you visit all the altars;
Nor lying prostrate, nor spreading out your hands
Before the sanctuaries, nor sprinkling the altars
With the blood of animals and a procession of prayers,
But to look on everything with a mind at peace.
When we look up to the temples of the sky
And the ether fast above all the glittering stars
And as we think of the course of the sun and the moon,
Then to add to the other ills which weigh us down
This fear also begins to raise its head:
That the power of the gods may be unlimited
And it may be that which sets the stars in motion.
It is poverty of reason troubles the mind
And we wonder about the origins of the world
And whether it may not end, and the walls of the world
Not be able to stand this motion much longer;
Or whether, the gods having rendered them eternal,
They might go gliding on and on for ever,
Defying for ever the strong power of time.

Besides, whose mind is not contracted with fear
Because of the gods? whose body is not afraid

169

When the parched earth trembles under the lightning
And great rumblings of thunder cross the sky?
Are not whole nations terrified? Kings may be proud
But they stoop quickly enough when they fear the gods,
Afraid that for some one crime or even a word
The day of reckoning may suddenly have come.
When wind and waves exhibit all their violence
And sweep before them the commander of the fleet,
To say nothing of his legions and elephants,
Does he not seek the mercy of the gods
And timidly ask for a lull and favourable winds?
It does no good, for the fierce hurricane
Often carries him to the shallows of death all the same:
So much a secret force kicks men around
And tramples on all the splendid rods and axes
Which it seems to treat with something less than respect.
And finally, when the whole world rocks under our feet
And cities are shaken and fall or threaten to do so,
What wonder if human beings abase themselves
And hand over everything which happens here
To the power of the gods and let them rule everything?

Next copper and gold and iron were discovered,
Lumps of silver, and what could be done with lead,
When fire consumed huge forests in a blaze
On high mountains, either started by lightning,
Or because, when they were waging war in the woods,
Men brought in fire to terrify their enemies;
Or because, seeing the soil was fertile, they wanted
To open up new fields or make new pastures;
Or perhaps to drive out beasts and grow rich on the spoil,
For pits and fires were certainly used in hunting
Long before men had snares and packs of hounds.
However it happened, and whatever the cause of flames,
When the forests were crackling up from their very roots
So that the earth beneath was baked deep down,
Out of its burning veins there trickled a stream
Of silver and gold and copper and lead, and collected
In hollow places: and when men saw it set,
When the fire had gone, and shine with its brilliant colours,
They were taken with it and picked up the smooth shining
                                                    pieces

And found they had taken the shape of the dips they had
run in.
Then it occurred to men that they could melt metals
And let them run into any mould they liked;
After which they could be made as sharp and fine as they
pleased
By hammering and drawing out the points;
So they made tools with which they could cut down forests,
Trim the wood and smooth it into planks
And finally pierce it and bore holes.

At first they set about using silver and gold
As well as the much stronger metal, copper:
They proved no good, it was found that they simply bent
And could not stand up half as well to the work.
Then copper was more valued and gold neglected
As something useless you couldn't put a good point on:
Now copper has gone down and what men honour is gold.
So time as it runs on changes every fashion
And what was once valued attracts no honour at last.
Then something else comes along, which was disregarded
But now is more sought after from day to day
And everyone praises that and says it is marvellous.

It is easy now, Memmius, to find out for yourself
In what way the nature of iron was discovered.
The original weapons were hands and nails and teeth
And stones and pieces of broken wood from the forest
And flames and fire, once the use of them was known.
The value of iron came to light after that of copper
Which is easier to work and found in greater abundance.
It was with copper men ploughed, it was with copper
Men threw themselves into battle and dealt out wounds,
Acquired cattle and fields as well: for those who are naked
And have no arms give way to those who are armed.
Gradually the iron sword became popular
And a sickle of copper became ridiculous;
It was with iron that men tore up the ground
And its general use made chances in war more equal.

The habit of armed men mounting on horseback
And guiding the horse with one hand while they fight with
the other

Is older than risking the battle from a two-horsed chariot,
And two-horsed chariots came before chariots-and-four
Where the armed man is protected by scythes on the wheels.
Later came elephants with towers on their backs
And trunks like snakes: the Carthaginians trained them
To take wounds calmly and make the enemy panic.
Discord invented one device after another
To make war ghastly to the nations engaged in it;
From day to day the horrors of war increased.
Men even tried to use bulls as part of the army
And to loose fierce boars into the midst of the enemy;
Some went to battle preceded by powerful lions
With armed keepers to keep them under control
Who were supposed to guide and keep them in chains.
It didn't work; they got excited by carnage
And caused confusion a little too indiscriminately
And their fearful manes popped up in unsuitable places:
There was no controlling the horses, and no certainty
That they would continue to advance on the enemy.
The lionesses threw their excited bodies
In all directions and would attack whomever they met,
While others they would unexpectedly take from the rear
And pin them down to the ground or leave them wounded,
Or fasten them with their teeth and claws.
The bulls would toss and trample on their owners
And rip the bellies of horses from below
Or at least churn up the ground and look very threatening.
The boars would tear up their allies with their tusks,
Dyeing with blood the weapons broken upon them
And shaking up both infantry and cavalry.
For the horses would shy away from the side where the
tusk was
Or stand on their hind legs and try to take to the air:
That didn't work either, for their tendons were often
snapped
And they came tumbling down in a heavy fall.
These animals which they thought so domesticated
Got a little heated with all that was going on,
The wounding, the shouting, the flight, the terror, the
tumult;
It was quite impossible to collect even a few of them,
The whole menagerie flew in various directions

As elephants now when they are deeply wounded
Will bolt and often damage their own side.
That was how things were managed: but I find it hard to
                                        believe
That men could not have seen there would be trouble
Before they brought so much of it on themselves:
But they did what they did not so much in the hope of
                                        winning
As to make their enemies suffer and die in the process
When they themselves had too few men and perhaps
                                        inferior weapons.

Before they were woven, clothes were tied together:
Weaving comes after iron; to make looms requires tools
Without which men could not have made spindles and
                                        beams
And other parts of the spinning and weaving equipment.
It was naturally men who first learned to work up the wool,
Long before women, because they are better at everything,
Altogether more skilful and industrious;
But they took to agriculture and scorned making clothes –
They handed that job over to the women
And themselves took up the harder kinds of work,
Making their hands and bodies hard in the process.

The first idea of sowing seeds and of grafting
Came as one might expect from nature herself
Since berries and acorns fallen from the trees
Would give a swarm of young shoots when the season came
                                        round;
From that would come the idea of inserting grafts
And planting saplings here and there in the fields:
Then men would try something else in their charmed acres
And see an improvement in the wild fruits they grew there
In proportion as they coaxed and tended the ground.
As time went on they forced the edge of the forest
Back to the mountains and cultivated the valleys;
Meadows, lakes, streams, fields of corn and pleasant
                                        vineyards
Covered the hillsides and levels and soon the olive
Showed its blue edge running along the boundaries
As it spread over ups and downs and across the plains,

Just as now you can see the various agreeable colours
Of the fruit-trees decorating the coloured plantations
And the shrubs which mark off one plot from another.

The imitation of birdsong by the voice
Came long before the singing of measured verses
Which men in time learned to make to please their ears.
The whistling of breezes through the hollow reeds
Taught country people to blow into hollow stalks;
Bit by bit they learned to make the plaintive sounds
Which come from the pipe when the fingers bring it to life;
A discovery of secluded groves and woods
And the pastures where shepherds spent their empty days.
These things they would find soothing and delightful
When full of food: for then all things are pleasant.
Often they lay stretched out on the soft grass
Beside a stream and under the shade of a tree.
They took their pleasures at very little cost,
Especially when the weather was good and the season
Provided them with a suitable carpet of flowers.
There were games then and talk and friendly laughter;
It was then that the country muse was at her best.
Head and shoulders were decorated with garlands
Of flowers and leaves, which prompted various amusements
Including some clumsy dancing out of time
And heavy feet stamping rather hard on the earth,
The occasion of smiles and a great deal of laughter
— For everything was new, and that is exhilarating.
There was consolation for the absence of sleep
In the miscellaneous voices getting the song wrong
As someone ran his crooked lip over the pipes.
We have these amusements ourselves still in the evenings
But have learned to keep better time though that does not
make us
Listen to what we hear with any more pleasure
Than those country people got from their entertainments.

For whatever we have, if we haven't known anything
pleasanter,
Will seem to us absolutely the best there is;
Yet generally, with the discovery of something better,
It loses its value and our feelings about it change.

So acorns came to be scorned; and nobody wanted a bed
Of grass and leaves such as was thought comfortable once.
Garments made of skins were sneered at in time
Although I think the invention of them was envied
And probably cost the original wearer his life;
Though, torn to pieces and covered with blood by the
                                           murderers,
The garment they stole probably wasn't much use to them.

Then it was skins, now it is gold and purple
People think so much of they will go to war for it:
In my opinion the current error is worse.
Cold was torture to naked men and a sheepskin
Did something for them: but there is no disadvantage
In managing without purple or gold or patterns
Since ordinary clothes give all the cover we need.
It seems the human race likes to labour for nothing
And always to spend its time in empty cares.
Why? because people don't understand that possession is
                                           limited
And that there is pleasure in it only up to a point.
It is this which has carried people drifting along
Until they have stirred up all the storms of war.

But those vigilant watchers of the turning sky,
The sun and the moon, filling all with their light,
Taught men the seasons came round always in order
And that everything happens in accordance with a pattern.

People had long learned to build themselves strong places
And long divided up and tilled the land;
They had made the sea blossom with ships under sail
And found out all about allies and making treaties
— All this before the poets began
To hand things down, writing had only just been invented:
That is why we cannot look back very far
Except so far as reasoning allows us inferences.

Navigation, the cultivation of fields,
Defences, laws, arms, roads, clothes, all the rest,
Even to all the elegances of life,
Poems, pictures, marvellous statues, all are the outcome

Of practice and indefatigable minds
For all have been achieved little by little.
So it is time produces different discoveries
And reason gradually brings them into the daylight.
So step by step the mind of man grew clearer
Until the arts reached their perfection.

BOOK VI

After a further eulogy of Epicurus, the poet examines various atmospheric phenomena — thunder, lightning, waterspouts, clouds and rain. An account of terrestial phenomena follows — earthquakes, why the sea does not overflow, the eruption of volcanoes, the flooding of the Nile, the magnet, and finally the spread of disease. This leads to the description of plague in Athens with which the poem ends.

The first to bring corn to uneasy mortals
In times past was the famous city of Athens
Which made life anew and instituted laws:
And first brought delicious consolation to life
When she gave birth to the man of genius so extraordinary
That everything came from a mouth devoted to truth
So that, even now he is dead, his divine discoveries
Spread abroad, carrying his glory to the sky.

For when he saw that whatever men's needs demanded
So far as may be, to keep their lives in safety,
Was there at hand already for their use,
That men had all they could want in the way of wealth
And honour and praise, and pride in successful children
Yet still at home were perpetually disquieted
And that the mind was enslaved by all its bitter complaints,
He understood that the trouble was in the container
And because of some flaw in it everything would go bad
Whatever excellent things were put into it:
Partly because there were holes and things flowed through
them
And there was no possibility of filling it up;
And partly because what did get in was spoiled
So to speak by the nauseous taste there was inside.

The truth was what he used to purify hearts with
And he set a limit to fear as to desire;
He explained what it is that all of us really want
And showed us the way along a little path
Which makes it possible for us to go straight there;
He showed what evils there are in human affairs

177

And how they were brought about by the force of nature,
Popping up by chance or because nature worked that way;
And he showed how best to encounter each of these
                                    difficulties
And proved that the human race was generally vain
In the way it ruminated its gloomy thoughts.
For just as children are afraid of the dark
Their elders are as often as not afraid in the light
Of things which there is as little cause to fear
As those which children imagine to frighten themselves.
These grown-up terrors are also no more than shadows
And yet they are nothing that the sunlight can dissipate:
What is needed is the rational study of nature
And that is why I want to continue this discourse.

Since I have explained that the structure of the world
Is mortal and that the heavens must begin and end;
And have made clear most of what happens or can happen
In the universe, now listen to what remains.
When once I get into my poetic chariot
I have every hope of arriving. Oh, there are obstacles
But I turn them upside-down with my inspiration.

There are other phenomena men perceive in the universe
Which often cause their minds acute suspense
And make them cringe before the fear of the gods,
Pressing themselves to the ground, because ignorance
Of the causes forces them to attribute everything
To the power of the gods, who, they suppose, are in charge.
Even those who have taken the point that the gods are
                                    indifferent
Sometimes wonder how the whole affair is managed
And are especially concerned about things above them
Which they see rolling around so high in the heavens.
Once more they revert to the ancient superstitions
And take those terrible masters they think all-powerful,
Not knowing that there are some things which can happen
And some which cannot, that every power is limited
By the system itself, and that everything has an end.
Their reason is blind and leads them wandering on.

Unless you put out of your head any suggestion
That the gods have attributes inconsistent with their peace,

178

They—since you have made light of their sanctified powers—
Will do you harm: not that the power of the gods
Can be so outraged that they will want to punish you
But you will imagine that they, who are really at peace,
Can find themselves rolling in billows of anger,
Nor will you be able to receive in suitable peace
The images which flow from their holy bodies
Into men's minds and announce the shape of divinity.
So you see to what kind of life such thoughts will lead you.

Though many reflections have already started from me
There is still much I must put into this elegant verse-form
If the truest reason is to drive such thoughts away.
We must grasp the meaning of certain heavenly phenomena;
My poem must treat of storms and flashes of lightning,
Their effects, as well as the causes which bring them about.
You are not to calculate fearfully from what quarters
The flying fire has come, or in what directions
It has turned, and in what way it has entered
Behind closed doors, done what it will, and escaped;
These are things which, if you do not understand causes,
You are apt to attribute to the power of the gods.
Be good enough, ingenious Muse, Calliope,
Who gives relief to men and pleasure to gods,
To indicate the way to the winning conclusion;
If I follow you no doubt I shall be applauded.

First, when thunder shakes the blue of the sky,
It is because high-flying clouds come together,
Crashing as they are driven by opposing winds:
The sound does not come from the serene part of the
                                                    heavens,
But wherever the army of clouds is massed and thickest
The snorts and growls are the most often heard.

Clouds cannot be made of anything so solid
As stone or timber, nor of anything so rarefied
As mists are or, say, flying bodies of smoke.
If they were they should either sink under their own weight
Like stones or, like smoke, they would fail to keep together
And would not be able to carry snow and hail.

At times they sound across the depths of the sky
Like the clashing noises which sometimes in great theatres
Sounds from the canvas stretched between the beams;
At times the clouds are torn by the petulant winds
With a noise which resembles the crackling of tearing paper:
You often hear something of that kind in thunder
Or when the wind whirls round a flapping garment
Or catches flying paper and beats it in the air.

It sometimes happens that clouds do not meet directly,
As it were head on, but slide past one another
And as they go graze one another's bodies;
That gives a sort of dry sound on the ears
And long drawn out until they have passed each other.

Another way in which everything seems to be shaken
By a shock of thunder and suddenly torn apart
So that the walls of the world seem about to crack
Is when a squall has suddenly come together
And buried itself in the clouds and, there shut in,
Turning itself round and round in a whirlwind,
Hollows the clouds and forces the crust to thicken,
Then, when its violence has weakened the outer cover,
With a terrifying crash it breaks it up.
Hardly surprising, since a little bag of air
Often goes off with a bang when it explodes.

Another reason why winds, when they blow through the
                                                    clouds,
Make a noise, is this: we often see clouds with branches
Carried roughly this way and that: it is just as when
The north wind blows through the densest part of the forest
And the leaves make a rushing noise and the branches crack.

It sometimes happens too that the force of the wind
Is such that a cloud breaks by direct attack.
What a blast can do is plain enough to the eye
For here where the wind is gentler we see none the less
Great trees pulled up by the roots, deep though they are.
And there are waves in clouds which so to speak roar
As they break heavily: just as happens in rivers
Which are big enough, or the sea when the surf breaks in.

Sometimes when lightning falls from cloud to cloud
It suddenly comes to one that is full of water
And the fire dies and as it dies cries out,
As iron red-hot from the furnace will suddenly hiss
When we take and plunge it straight into cold water.
If the cloud which the lightning strikes proves to be drier
Instead the fire catches and we hear blazing:
As happens when a hill which is covered with laurel
Catches alight and then huge gales sweep over it;
And nothing burns with a fiercer crackling sound
Than the Delphic laurel of Phoebus, licked by the flames.

And it often happens that there is a cracking of ice
And rattle of hail in clouds as they move aloft
When the wind crams them together until they break,
Mountains of storm-clouds with a sliding mass of hail.

There is lightning when the clouds as they clash together
Strike out elements of fire, as when stone strikes on stone
Or on iron, for you see the light spring out then
And fire scatter itself in brilliant sparks.
But our ears perceive the thunder only after
The eyes have seen the lightning, for sounds always move
More slowly than things which present themselves to the
                                                    eye.
You can see that, watching from a distance while someone
Strikes a tree with an axe; you will see the blow fall
Before the sound of it strikes upon your ears.
Exactly the same with lightning, which we see
Before we hear the thunder; they occur together,
Produced by a single cause, the collision of clouds.

As to how places are suddenly tinged
By lightning from the clouds, quick, tempestuous flashes:
When the wind has gone into a cloud and turned about
Making it hollow and thickening up the walls
As I have explained, the cloud grows hot from the movement,
As everything does until it bursts into flame;
A ball of lead which goes far will spin till it melts.
So the wind, grown hot, when cutting through a black cloud,
Scatters elements of fire pressed out by the force;
It is these which produce the winking flashes of flame:

181

Then the sound follows, which is slower to reach the ears
Than the visible matter is to reach the eye.
This happens when clouds are closely packed and piled
High above one another in a great cumulus.

You should not be misled by what we see from below
Which is their width, rather than the superstructure.
Consider, when the winds have carried the clouds
Like mountains through the air in a slanting course
Or when you see them pile one on top of the other
On the sides of great mountains and pressing down from
                                                    above,
Completely at rest and the winds are everywhere buried:
You will then be able to see how huge they are
With caves as it were hollowed from hanging rocks.
And when a storm has gathered and the winds have filled
                                                    them,
They growl with indignation at being shut up;
Their language is like that of wild beasts in their lairs.
Now this way, now that, they send their snorts through
                                                    the clouds
And turn them around in the clouds' hollow furnaces
Until they tear from the cloud and we see the flashes.

Another cause of the golden colour of fire
That flies down sometimes so swiftly to the ground
Is that the clouds themselves have many elements
Of fire: for when they are without moisture
They generally are of a brilliant flame colour.
Moreover they take many elements from the sun
And for this reason grow red and spill fire.
Therefore when the wind drives them on and presses them
Together into one place, some elements fall,
Squeezed out, and then you see the flashes of colour.

There is lightning too when the clouds in the sky are
                                                    scattered.
For when the wind draws them apart and breaks them
Some elements must fall out and so make lightning.
It is then that the flashes are accompanied by noise,
There is no terror and no sign of disturbance.

As to the nature of lightning, that can be seen
From the way it strikes and the traces of heat it leaves,
The marks of burning, the air smelling of sulphur.
These are signs of fire, not of wind or rain.
Besides, the roofs of houses are often set alight
And flames rage through the inside of the buildings.
This sort of fire is the most subtle there is,
Composed by nature of highly mobile elements
Which are extremely small, so that nothing can stop it.
That is why lightning will pass through the walls of houses
As the sound of voices will; it passes through metal and
                                                    stone;
And in a flash melts either bronze or gold.
It can make wine disappear without harming the vessel,
Which it does by loosening the texture of what it strikes
So that the clay becomes porous suddenly,
The effect of the heat, which then gets inside the vessel
And decomposes the elements of the wine:
That is more than the heat of the sun seems able to do
And gives a notion of the force of the lightning
Which is much more mobile and more masterful.

Now how does it come into being? And how does it get
The force that enables it to crack strong towers?
To throw down houses and tear up beams and rafters?
To heave up and shift the public monuments?
To seek out men and strike them down like cattle?
How does it manage to do such things as this?
I will proceed at once with my explanation.
Lightning must come from the densest clouds
When they are piled up high: for it never comes
From a clear sky or when the clouds are light.
The matter is clear enough from the manifest facts:
It comes when the clouds pile up in all directions
Across the sky, and we think that the shadows of Acheron
Have filled up all the hollows of the sky:
A terrifying night seems to have begun
And the faces of black fear are hanging over us
When the storm begins to gather its thunderbolts.

It often happens that a black cloud over the sea
Falls into the waves like a river of pitch

And is carried on with its shadows, bringing with it
A black storm heavy with lightning and squalls,
Itself being first of all full of fire and winds;
So that men on shore are afraid and make for shelter.
We must conclude that the storm above our heads
Has deep reaches. How otherwise would such blackness
Cover the earth, if clouds were not built up
So as to cause the sun to disappear:
And how could such rains fall from these same clouds
To make rivers overflow and flood the plains
If the structure of clouds did not reach far into the ether?

For everything there is full of winds and fires
With thunder here and there and flashes of lightning.
There must be many elements of heat,
As I have shown, in clouds that are hollowed out
And the clouds must take in more from the rays of the sun.
As soon as the wind, having collected the clouds
In a particular place, has forced out elements
Of heat and mingled itself with that same fire
It whirls about, caught in a narrow space,
Until it has pointed the thunderbolt as in a furnace;
For it takes fire both from its own mobility
And from the heat of the adjacent fire.
So when the wind has grown extremely hot
And the rushing flame lights up, the lightning is ready
To cut through the cloud and so the heat is carried
Alive into the world and illumines everything:
The dull thunderclap follows, and seems to crash down
From the heavens which have the appearance of cracking
                                    asunder.
Then a trembling seizes the earth and a murmur
Runs heavily through the sky; and the whole storm almost
Trembles as if it were shaken by the roaring:
The shock is followed by explosions of rain
So that the whole sky seems to turn into rain
And pouring down it calls back the time of the flood:
There is such a breaking of cloud and such bursts of wind
And the sound of thunder flies out of the burning strokes.

Sometimes from outside a wind of great violence
Falls on a cloud which is hot with a thunderbolt;

When it tears it apart, the fire at once falls out
In the vortex we are accustomed to call a thunderbolt.
The wind goes on and does the same elsewhere.

Sometimes it happens that a wind without any fire
Catches alight in the course of its long journey
During which it has lost some heavy elements
Which could not keep pace with it as it tore through the
                                                                    air;
And at the same time collected some smaller elements
Which make fire as they mix with it in their flight.
It is much the same as when a ball of lead
Grows hot as it glides through the air while shedding its cold
Elements and picking up fire as it goes along.

The force of collision may also stir up fire
When the shock comes from a wind which is not ignited;
For when it has struck against something strongly enough
Elements of heat can emerge from the wind itself
As well as from the object it strikes upon;
As when we strike stone with iron, fire flies out.
The metal may well be cold, but none the less
The elements of heat are called out by the blow:
So anything can be set on fire by a thunderbolt
If it is readily combustible.
The wind cannot indeed be entirely cold
If it has come with so much force from above;
And if its flight has not made it catch alight
It arrives slightly warm and with some admixture of fire.

The mobility of lightning, the force of its stroke
And the speed with which it rushes to its descent
Come from the fact that it collects in the clouds
And makes a great effort before it gets away.
When the cloud cannot hold the swelling impetus
The force is squeezed out and flies at a marvellous rate
As missiles are hurled from the most powerful siege-engines.

There is also the fact that its elements are small
And light, and things of that nature are scarcely resistible,
So it finds its way through even the tiniest openings:
There is therefore very little that can hold it back

And it slips through objects at remarkable speed.
Then, anything which has weight will tend to go
                                        downwards
And when to that tendency an impulsion is added
The speed is doubled and the impetus increased
So that it hits whatever gets in its way
Faster and more violently and so runs on.

Then since it comes from a distance it must gain speed
Which increases in proportion to the distance
And so augments its force and the strength of its impact:
The effect of speed is that whatever elements go with it
Are carried together to a single point,
Their individual trajectories being swept aside.

It may be that as it goes it pulls from the air
Elements which will further increase its mobility.

Many things it passes through and leaves intact
Because the fire is fluid and finds the interstices.
Many others it breaks, because its elements
Fall precisely on the elements of the object.
Brass it easily melts, and gold it fuses
Instantaneously, because it is made of elements
Which are very small as well as extremely smooth,
And easily get inside those metals and when they are in
Undo all the links and loosen the connections.

It is in autumn with all its shining stars
That heaven and earth are most often shaken by lightning
And in the spring when all the flowers are out.
Winter lacks fire and summer has few winds
And the clouds at that time are hardly thick enough.
When the seasons are between the two extremes
All the causes of thunder are found together.
Those passages of the year have both cold and heat:
Both of which are needed for the making of thunder,
For that discord of nature in which the furious air
Rises in roaring waves of fires and winds.

The first hint of the heat and the last of the cold
Is the time of spring: things so dissimilar

Must be in conflict and there must be confusion.
And the last of the heat, mixed with the first of the cold,
Brings us to the season which we call autumn;
That is why these two periods are so rough.
No wonder at such times there is often thunder
And troublous storms drive up and down the sky
Since these are times when both sides are stirred to battle,
Flames on one side, on the other winds mixed with water.

This is the way to see the nature of thunder
And to understand how it produces its effects,
And not by reading books of Etruscan saws
To find out exactly what the gods are up to,
Where they have sent their fire from, or in what direction
It has turned, or in what manner it has entered
Behind closed doors, done what it will, and escaped,
Or what disasters from heaven thunder can bring.

If it is Jupiter and the other gods
Who shake the glittering sky with their terrible crashes
And if they can hurl their fires wherever they like
Why don't they strike at people who have committed .
Revolting crimes and make them spew out flames?
Stick them through the middle and make examples of them?
Why must it be instead the innocent,
People whose consciences are as clear as noon-day,
Who get caught up in the whirlwind of heavenly fire?

And why do they bother to throw their bolts in the desert?
Is it for exercise and to tone up their muscles?
Why do they waste their ammunition on earth
Instead of keeping it for the Old Man's enemies?

And then, why is it never from a clear sky
That Jupiter throws his bolts and makes his noise?
Perhaps he waits till the clouds provide him with cover
To go down himself and take his aim from close quarters?
Then why does he hit the sea? Has he something against
The waves, or finds so much water not to his taste?

Again, if he wants us to get out of the way,
Why won't he let us see where he's going to throw?

Or if he wants to catch us unawares
Why does he make so much noise that we have warning?
Why does he start with darkness and rumbling and
                                                    grumbling?

And how does he manage to throw from so many directions
At the same time? It would be very rash to assert
That several bolts have never been loosed simultaneously.
It happens often enough, indeed it must happen
That just as rain falls in a number of places
At the same time, there can be several thunderbolts.

Lastly, why does he choose to smash up sanctuaries,
Even his own shrines, with his fatal bolts?
Make cracks in the statues of gods from top to toe?
And even strike images put up in his honour?
Why does he go for high places, why do we so often
See evidence of his fire on the tops of mountains?

After what has been said it is easy to understand
What the Greeks call presters and we refer to as waterspouts
Which come down from above into the sea.
Sometimes it happens that what looks like a pillar
Descends from the sky into the sea while all around
The water boils and is whipped up by the wind:
And any ship which is caught in that agitation
Very soon finds itself in the greatest danger.
This occurs when wind imprisoned in a cloud
Tries to break out but does not quite succeed
And instead presses down in a way that gives the appearance
Of a pillar gradually descending into the sea
As if an arm were pushing the cloud from the inside
And gradually extending it till it touches the water:
When it does break the cloud the force of the wind rushes
                                                            out
Into the sea and produces tremendous boiling.
The whirlwind in effect descends and brings with it
The elastic and extensible skin of the cloud:
As soon as this mass touches the sea's surface
The whole thing plunges into the water
Stirring it up with great force and causing the boiling.

It sometimes happens that a whirlwind gets caught up in
                                                    clouds,
Gathers up particles of cloud from the air
And imitates a prester coming down from the sky;
When it finishes on land and is broken open
It spews an immense eddy, you might say a hurricane;
But that happens rarely because of course on land
Mountains get in the way, so it happens more often
On the vast stretch of the sea, under the open sky.

Clouds are formed when a number of cloud-elements,
Which are rather rough, come together in the sky;
They are of a kind which have only a loose hold on one
                                                    another
But none the less manage to stay together.
They first form themselves into small clouds;
Then these absorb one another, and when they come
                                                    together
You get the large clouds which are carried on by the wind
To the point where an immense storm is gathered.

The nearer mountain-tops are to the sky,
The more they all the time give off a sort of smoke;
There is a darkness composed of mist and cloud
Because when clouds are beginning to form
And are still so thin as to be invisible, the winds
Carrying them force them up to the top of a mountain;
There, when a considerable mass has collected
And is dense enough for the clouds to become visible,
They rise from the peak into the upper air.
That these places are windy is plain to our senses
Whenever we take the trouble to climb a high mountain.

The surface of the sea gives off a number of particles
As you can see from what happens to clothes hung by the
                                                    shore,
Which always collect a certain amount of moisture:
Just so many particles arise
From the surface of the sea to increase the size of clouds:
The two kinds of moisture are much alike.
Besides, we see mists rising from all rivers
And indeed from the ground; these exhalations are then

189

Carried aloft and cover the sky with darkness
And coming together gradually form high clouds:
For the heat of the ether with its stars presses down on them
And by condensing them forms rain-clouds below the blue.

It can happen also that elements which make clouds
Come into the sky from the regions beyond it.
There are innumerable elements, as I have explained,
And space is infinite: I have shown how swiftly
The particles move, in how short a time
They manage to traverse incredible distances.
So it is no wonder it takes so short a time
For storm and shadow to cover high mountains,
The seas and the land, and to weigh down upon them;
On all sides, through the pores of the upper air.
And so to speak through all the vents of the great world,
The elements are able to enter and go out.

Now one moment while I explain how rain-water collects
High up in the clouds, and how it comes down in showers.
First I will prove how the particles of water
In the clouds themselves and rising from other things
Come together and grow as the cloud grows:
The clouds and the water contained in them increase
                                        reciprocally
Just as our bodies produce at the same time as our blood
Our sweat and all the liquid of the organism.
Clouds also take in moisture from the sea
When, like so many fleeces hung out to dry,
The clouds are carried over the surface by the wind.
In a similar manner moisture from all the rivers
Is carried into the clouds: and when many water-particles
Have been assembled in them from all directions
The close-packed clouds try to discharge the liquid
In two ways: the force of the wind upon them
And their own density, results in a certain pressure
From up above, which causes the showers to fall:
Or else when the clouds are scattered by the wind
Or dispersed under the force of the sun's rays
They release their moisture, and drip, in the way that wax
Over a hot fire melts and turns to liquid.

But the rain is violent when the clouds are violently pressed
At the same time by the wind and their own weight;
And it is sure to last for a long time
When a great number of water particles is set in motion
And cloud after cloud pressed one on top of the other
Is streaming along from all quarters, and the earth
Is breathing moist exhalations back at the cloud.

If, at such a moment, the sunshine breaks through
Just opposite the rain which drops from the clouds,
You see all the colours of the rainbow.

As to the other things produced in the sky
And those which develop within the clouds themselves,
All of them, snow, winds, hail and icy frost
As well as the original force which causes the freezing
And in places stops the rivers in their courses,
It is easy to understand how they are created
And all the laws which determine their existence
Once you have understood how the elements operate.

Now take a look at what causes earthquakes:
But first of all you must understand that the earth,
Further down as well as nearer the surface
Is full of windy caverns and lakes and chasms;
There are great rocks lying about, and precipices,
Under the skin of the earth there are even rivers
Submerging rocks which throw up violent waves,
For the earth must surely be like itself through and through.

If that is the state of things which obtains below
The earth above will tremble when underneath
Things fall to ruin, as great caves fall in time.
Whole mountains fall and from the stupendous shock
The tremor spreads itself in all directions;
Quite naturally, for houses at the side of a road
Shake when a wagon passes, though it does not weigh much
And the wagons themselves jump when even a little stone
Jolts on the iron tyres of one of the wheels.

It happens too, when a great mass of soil
Loosened by time, slides into a gigantic lake,

That the shaking of the water will shake the land,
As a vessel is not at rest, unless the liquid
Contained in it, itself is perfectly still.

Again, when the wind in the hollow parts of the earth
Collects itself and bears down on one point
And pushes against the cave with all its might,
The earth itself is tipped in the same direction:
Then, above ground, the buildings standing upon it,
Especially those which are of considerable height,
Tip over a little in the same direction;
The timbers stick out and are ready to fall.
Yet men are afraid to think that the whole world
Will have its own time of destruction and ruin
Although they see the whole mass waiting to fall!
If the winds never paused for breath no power could stop
The slide of everything towards destruction.
But as they sometimes pause and sometimes blow,
Resting occasionally or stopped by obstacles,
There are more often threats than actual disasters;
The earth rocks one way then recovers herself,
Tumbles and then retrieves her former position.
That is the reason all buildings tremble,
Most at the top, less lower, at the base hardly at all.

There is another cause of major earthquakes.
A wind, an enormous mass of air which has come
Either from outside or from within the earth,
Hurls itself into all sorts of hollow places
And rages and roars at first in the great caverns,
Whirling round in them, until at last its force
Breaks a way out and so splits up the earth
And leaves a yawning chasm where it blew.
That is what happened in Syria, in Sidon
And again at Aegium on the Peloponnese,
Both towns were destroyed by outbreaks of wind and
                                        earthquakes.
Many other walled cities have fallen thus
In earthquakes, many towns have sunk in the sea
And disappeared with all their inhabitants.

If it does not split the earth, the force of the wind,
Penetrating through all the cracks and crannies,

Causes a sort of shudder and everything trembles
As cold will shake us when it gets into our limbs
And causes them to tremble whether we like it or not.
Cities then suffer from a double terror,
There is fear of falling roofs and fear underfoot
That the subterranean caverns will be destroyed.
Is nature about to open a great abyss
Which she will fill up with a terrible pile of ruins?
Let men think if they can that heaven and earth are somehow
Permanent structures exempt from all decay;
Yet sometimes they are faced with this sort of peril
Which pricks their confidence with a particular fear
And they think the ground may fall away under their feet
Into a gulf, and everything follow after
Until the world is nothing but ruins and chaos.

Now I must explain why the sea doesn't grow.
People are astonished that it doesn't get any bigger
Since there is such a flow of water into it;
All the rivers after all end up there.
You must add the effect of all the rains and storms
Which splash and stream over both land and sea
And the sea's own springs: yet in fact these many additions
To so great a bulk will hardly amount to a drop:
This is itself a reason for not being too astonished.

Besides, the sun draws off a lot with its heat,
As we see that clothes which are hung out dripping wet
Dry quickly enough in the burning rays of the sun.
But the oceans are many and stretched out far and wide:
So even though the sun may take very little
From any particular part of the vast surface
It amounts to quite a lot for the whole area.

The winds also must carry off some moisture
As they sweep across the surface;
We see how roads will often dry up in a night —
The same with slushy mud which turns quite hard.

Besides, I have shown that the clouds themselves carry off
Not a little moisture from the surface of the sea
And scatter it here and there all over the earth
When it rains in the lands to which wind carries the clouds.

Finally, since the earth is of its nature porous
And joined to the sea wherever there is a shore
It must be that, as the sea gets water from inland
So the land receives some seepage from salt water:
The stinging liquid is filtered and loses its salt
And flows back to the sources of rivers and so
Returns once more, now sweetened, over the land
Along the channels the streams have already worn.

Now I will explain how it is that the jaws of Mount Etna
From time to time emit such an eddy of fire.
It is no ordinary scourge, this storm of flames.
It raged as it would over the fields of Sicily,
The neighbouring peoples turned in that direction
As the whole sky was filled with smoke and sparks
And as they watched their hearts were terrified
At the new disasters they feared were in preparation.

In matters such as these you must take a wide view
And a long, long look at things in every direction,
And remember that the sum of things is infinite
So that our sky is a tiny part of the whole;
It is indeed a much smaller part proportionately
Than a man considered as part of the whole earth.
As long as you keep that point clearly in mind
You will spare yourself a good deal of astonishment.

For which of us thinks it strange that a man should be sick
With fever burning and shaking all his body
Or some other pain attacking one of his limbs?
He might suddenly have a swollen toe or a toothache
Or else a pain might suddenly pierce his eyes;
The holy fire breaks out, twists round the body,
Burns what it seizes on in this part or that:
There are indeed enough elements of many things
And the earth and the sky have enough of sickness and pain
To make up a plague of terrible proportions.
So it is, we must suppose, that our earth and sky
Are supplied with enough things out of the infinite
To set the earth in a moment shaking and rocking
Or a hurricane tearing over both land and sea,
To fill Etna with fire and light up the sky:

For indeed that happens and the sky itself can burn
As rainstorms fall more heavily whenever
There is a concentration of elements of water.

No doubt the fire which burns in Etna is huge.
The largest river a man has seen is always
The biggest one that there is: and so with a tree
Or a man: it is the same with everything,
The biggest one one has seen is thought gigantic.
Yet all that, with the sky, the earth and the sea
Are nothing when you consider the sum of things.

But I must get down to the point of explaining
How it is that flames, whipped up of a sudden, leap
From the furnaces of Etna. The whole mountain
Is hollow, supported throughout by basalt arches.
In all these caverns there is wind and air:
When this grows hot and heats the rocks and earth
Beating about wherever it touches them,
It strikes out from them fire in rapid tongues,
Then rises and flies up straight through mountain gorges.
So it carries its heat afar and scatters its ashes
And black,thick smoke is poured out in the air;
It hurls out rocks of an impressive size:
Can you doubt that all this comes from a gale of wind?

Besides, the sea, bathing the foot of the mountains,
Breaks against it and then sucks back the water.
From the shore the caves run up under the volcano
Till they reach the mouth. This is the way the wind blows
Up from the sea when the water is withdrawn
And is breathed out, sending the waves up with it,
Casting up stones, carrying up clouds of sand.
For at the top of the mountain there are the craters
As the locals call them, or jaws and mouths, as we say.

There are phenomena for which it is not sufficient
To state one cause, though only one will be true.
For example, if from a considerable distance
You see a corpse on the ground, it is by running over
The possible causes of death you will find the true one.
You cannot say whether the man has died by the sword,

Through the cold, by sickness or perhaps by poison;
What we do know is that he must have died by one of them.
This method will serve us in a number of matters.

The Nile rises in summer and floods the fields,
The only river in Egypt which so behaves.
It irrigates Egypt when the weather is hottest,
Perhaps because in summer there are north winds
Blowing against its mouth — what they call the Etesians —
And they drive back the water or hold it back
So that it fills the channel and keeps it still:
For certainly these winds blow upstream; they come
Indeed from the icy region about the pole:
The river comes from the south, from a heat-laden country,
Through the races of men who are baked black by the sun,
And rises far away where the sun stands highest.

It is possible too that an accumulation of sand
Is caused by the waves which push against the current
When the sea driven by the wind throws the sand inshore.
That would have the effect of barring the river's way
And making the descent of the water less rapid.

It is possible also that at this season the rains
Are heavier at its source, for this is the time
When the north winds blow the clouds into that region:
When they are gathered there in the south they are
Driven against the high mountains and so to speak jammed
                                                    there
Which results in their being pressed so that rain is squeezed
                                                    out.

Perhaps also the river collects its water
High up in the mountains of Ethiopia
Where the sun shines on the snows and they melt down.

Now we come to the nature of those places
And lakes which go by the title of Avernus.
The origin of the name is simply that
These are places which are hostile to birds;
For when birds flying over reach these spots
They forget to flap their wings and so fall down

With limp necks on to the ground below
If they are over land, or into the water.

There is such a spot at Cumae where the mountains exhale
An acrid smell of sulphur and the springs steam sulphur.
Another is at Athens, within the walls,
At the top of the citadel, by the temple of Pallas herself:
You will never hear a crow call there in its flight
Not even when the altar is smoking with sacrifices:
It is not a matter of the anger of Pallas
Avenging herself on their vigilance, as the poets made out;
The nature of the place is enough to discourage them.
In Syria too there is said to be a place
Which is such that any animal entering upon it
At once falls down as if he were being sacrificed.
But all this happens entirely from natural causes
And the origin of the phenomenon is plain:
No need to believe that these are the gates of Orcus
Or that the infernal gods are attracting souls
From these regions down to the shores of Acheron;
As people believe that somehow the scent of stag
Will draw a poisonous serpent out of its hiding-place.
How far this is from a reasonable explanation
I will try to make clear by presenting the facts.

First I will repeat what I have said before,
That there are in the world elements of all kinds of things
Many of them life-giving but many on the other hand
Causing diseases and accelerating death:
Some of them suit some people better than others;
Their vital effect varies, as I have shown.
It is a question of different natures and different textures
And different elements in various creatures and objects.
Some of the elements cause damage through the ears,
Some are dangerous when they enter through the nose,
There are some which must on no account be touched,
Others not looked at, others noxious to the taste.
There are indeed many things which for a man
Are offensive to sense, both nauseous and oppressive.
Certain trees have an oppressive shade,
So much so that often they will give a headache
To a man who lies on the grass under them for long.

197

There is even a tree upon Mount Helicon
The smell of which is enough to kill a man.
These no doubt are elements rising out of the earth
Which has in itself a great many different kinds
Generally mixed up but sometimes given out separately.

When the lamp has been put out at night, if its acrid stench
Reaches his nostrils it will put to sleep at once
A man who is subject to epileptic fits.
A woman will fall into a heavy sleep
And her work fall from her hands, if she has smelt
Castor when she is having her period.
Many other substances have the effect
Of sending people to sleep or making them drowsy.
Then if you stay too long in a hot bath
When you are rather full, how easily
You find you have collapsed in the middle of it.
And how easily the smell and fumes of charcoal
Enter the brain, if you don't drink water beforehand!
And when a man is already weakened by fever
The fumes of wine fall on him like a blow.
Do you not see that sulphur is generated
In the earth, like bitumen with its deadly smell?
And where there is mining for veins of gold and silver
Which men will dig for deep down in the earth
What stenches arise, as at Scaptensula!
How deadly are the exhalations of gold mines!
You can see the ill effects in the miners' complexions.
Have you not heard and seen how short is the life
Of a miner compelled to remain at this terrible task?
All these exhalations come from the earth
And are breathed forth into the open light of day.

That must be how the Avernian places produce
Their fatal emanations which rise from the earth
And poison a good part of the sky above.
As soon as the wings of the bird have carried it there
It is attacked at once by an unseen poison
And falls on the place which produces the exhalation:
When it reaches the ground the same power takes away
Whatever life remains in the creature's limbs.
The exhalation produces a dizziness

But once plunged into the sources of the poison
The bird has no choice but to vomit out its life,
Surrounded as it is by so much that will harm it.

Sometimes the exhalations rising from Avernus
Displace the air between the birds and the earth
Leaving something which is very nearly a void;
Then when the birds come flying from other places
Quite suddenly it is as if their wings were limping,
Their effort on one side and the other is wasted.
And when their wings will no longer bear them up
The ordinary action of nature sends them down
And lying on the ground in the virtual emptiness
Their souls disperse through every pore of their bodies.

   .   .   .   .   .

The water in wells is colder in the summer
Because the earth is dilated in the heat
And the elements of warmth fly into the air.
The more completely the earth is drained of these elements
The colder the water hidden in the ground will grow.
On the other hand when the earth contracts in the cold
And hardens, it is as if in the course of contracting
It presses into the wells all the heat that it can.

It is said that the temple of Hammon has a spring,
Cold in daylight, which grows warm at night.
This naturally causes astonishment; people suppose
That it is heated by the sun shining under the earth
When all above is covered with terrible darkness:
But that is a long way certainly from the truth.
If the sun striking directly on the water
Cannot make it hot when shining on the upper side,
Although there is so much heat in the light from above,
How could it through the whole thickness of the earth
Warm up the water and make it as hot as it is?
Especially since we know that the rays of the sun
At their hottest scarcely go through the walls of a house.

What is the reason? It is that the earth is porous,
More so than usual, round about the fountain
Near which many elements of fire are concentrated.
When the night weeps down with its waves of dew

The earth at once grows cold and so contracts;
It is as if it were squeezed in a great hand,
Pressing into the spring all the elements of fire
Which thus make the water hot to the touch and tongue.
When the rising sun has loosened the earth
And caused it to dilate as the heat goes in,
The elements of fire go back where they came from
And the earth once more takes all the heat from the water:
That is why the spring cools off as the daylight comes.

Besides the rays of the sun play on the water
And it is rarefied in the dancing heat,
Losing in this way all its fiery elements.
The same thing happens with water containing frost,
It lets go, there is a thaw and the structure relaxes.

There is a cold spring which will light a piece of tow
If the tow is held over the surface of it:
A pine-torch will be ignited by those waters
And burn as it floats away wherever the wind goes:
This is because the water has numerous elements
Of heat from the earth itself at the bottom;
Many more rise up all the way through the basin
And find their way to the surface and into the air,
Though not enough to warm up the water itself.

The force which drives the elements through the water
To break out and assemble at the top
Is like the spring in the sea at Aradus
Where fresh water wells up and pushes away the brine;
And in many other places the sea will provide
What must be a welcome relief to thirsty sailors,
Sweet water as it were belched up through the salt.
That is how in this spring the elements burst through the
                                                     water
And well out into the tow: when they come together
Either in the tow or in the pine-torch, and stick,
They catch fire easily, the reason being
That those materials contain a number of fire elements.

Haven't you noticed that if you bring near a lamp
A wick that has just been extinguished, it catches alight

Before it touches the flame, as a torch does too?
Many things indeed catch fire at a distance,
Merely by heat without a touch of the flame
And that is what happens at that famous spring.

Another matter. I will explain on what principles
It is possible that the power of attracting iron
Should reside in the stone which the Greeks call the magnet
Because it comes from the country round Magnesia.
This stone is another wonder: it can hold a chain
Of several rings without any other support;
You can sometimes see as many as five or more,
One below the other and moving in a slight draught;
The first holds the second, the second the next and so on,
Each taking the tying force of the stone from the other
For the power of the magnet penetrates in this way.

In matters of this kind there are points to establish
Before we can explain the particular phenomenon;
It must be approached in a somewhat circuitous way:
All the more reason to ask you to be attentive.

First of all, from everything that we see
There must be an incessant diffusing stream
Of bodies which strike our eyes and provoke sight:
From some things there must be incessant smells,
As coolness from rivers, heat from the sun, spray from the
                                                        sea
Which eats away at walls that are near the shore
And the air is always full of streaming sounds.
A moist salt flavour comes into our mouths
When we are wandering about beside the sea.
If wormwood is mixed before our eyes,we can feel it:
And so from everything there are emanations
Which are dispersed from them in every direction;
This happens without respite or intermission
For our senses are always working and at any time
We can see and smell and hear the sound of things.

You will remember that in the first part of this poem
I explained that nothing is absolutely solid.
This is an important point in many connections

But especially in relation to the matter
I am about to explain: it must be made clear
Whatever is perceptible is composed of matter and emptiness.

First, it happens in caves that the rocks up above
Sweat with water which comes down drip by drip;
In the same way sweat oozes all over our bodies;
Our beards grow, as well as hair elsewhere on our bodies;
Food spreads through our veins and feeds us and makes us
grow
Down to the tips of fingers and toes and nails.
Cold will go through brass, we feel the heat through it,
In the same way we feel it pass through silver and gold
As we see when we hold a cup which is full of liquid.
Sounds will pass through the stone walls of houses
And smells and cold and heat and fire go through;
Fire will penetrate even something as strong as iron
And force the cuirass round a soldier's body.
Diseases also come to us from outside,
And storms which are begun in the sky and the earth
Disappear in the sky and earth again,
Because there is nothing which does not have interstices.

Next it must be remembered that all the elements
Discharged from things do not give the same sensation
Nor are they adapted for everything alike.
The sun will bake the earth and make it dry
But it thaws ice and makes the snows piled up
On high mountains melt away in its rays:
Wax is liquefied when it is placed in the heat
But skin and flesh are dried up and contracted.
Water hardens iron that has been in fire
But it softens skin and flesh which the heat has hardened.
The wild olive is as delightful to goats
As if it were flavoured with ambrosia and nectar
But man finds its leaves the bitterest of any.
The pig will run from marjoram and anything perfumed;
Such things are poison to those bristly animals
Though they are just the things that we delight in.
On the other hand though to us their mire is filth
The pigs apparently find it quite delightful
For they are never tired of rolling in it.

There is one more thing I should mention before I go on
To the main explanation I have in hand.
Many of the pores with which things are provided
Must be dissimilar from one another,
The different kinds with passages of different shapes.
Living creatures have more than one channel of sense;
Each channel receives the impressions appropriate to it;
Sound goes through one, taste is perceived through another
While smell again has its peculiar passages
Varying according to the tissue of the substance.
One substance will, as we have seen, drip through rock,
Another through wood; another will pass through gold
Or silver and another will pass through glass.
Images flow through one, heat through another,
Other substances each find ways which are quickest for
                                                    them.
This is due to the variety of pores or passages,
Which is considerable, as I have shown above.

These principles once stated and firmly established
As the basis on which the enquiry should proceed,
It is not at all difficult to demonstrate
The way in which iron is attracted by a magnet.
In the first place, there must flow from the stone
A vast number of elements which push aside
The air between the iron and the stone itself.
With this space emptied, a considerable vacuum is formed
Between the two, and the elements of the iron
Fall into it in a crowd; the effect of that is
That the ring itself follows, for the whole mass of iron moves.
No substance has its primal elements
More closely implicated than those of iron
Which is icy by nature. The less reason for astonishment,
As I said before, that a body of its elements
Cannot leave the iron to flow into the vacuum
Without the ring following. It follows until it arrives
At the stone, to which it adheres by invisible ties.
This can happen in any direction in which the vacuum
Is created, either from one side or from above:
The neighbouring elements are carried into it at once;
Not capable themselves of rising in the air,
They are set in motion by bombardment from elsewhere.

What renders this account the more probable
Is the existence of another factor which helps movement.
As soon as the air opposite the ring has become rarefied
And a vacuum has been created in the intervening space,
The air behind the ring so to speak pushes it forward.
Objects are always bombarded by the air around them;
In the present case this can drive the iron forward
Because there is an empty space ready to receive it.
The air accordingly pushes its way against the iron
And indeed into the recesses of its smallest parts
And so drives it forward as wind does the sails of a ship.

Finally every substance has air in its structure
Because everything has interstices in it and air
Surrounds and is in contact with everything.
In this case therefore the air concealed in the iron
Is stirred up and becomes extremely restless
And no doubt strikes against the ring from inside.
This gives a new impulsion in the direction
In which it was already moving, drawn by the vacuum.

Sometimes the iron is repelled by the stone;
Its habit is to fly from and follow it in turn.
I have seen iron rings from Samothrace leap up at a touch
And also iron filings dance about
In a brass basin when a magnet has been placed underneath,
So anxious does the iron seem to get away.
This disturbance is caused by the interposition of brass;
No wonder, for emanations from that metal
Get to the pores of the iron ahead of those
Which come from the magnet, and when they arrive
They find everything full and no way in.
They are therefore forced to dash against the surface of
the iron
And to beat upon it: the magnet repels the iron
And agitates through the brass the metal it would
otherwise attract.

It is not surprising that the emanations
Coming from the stone do not act the same way on other
things.
Some things resist because of their weight, as gold does,

Some because their substance is not dense enough and the
                                                    emanations
Go through without touching and so push upon nothing:
Wood appears to be a substance of this kind.
Iron is somewhere between the two;
It needs only a few elements of brass to acquire
The property of responding to magnetic influence.

These phenomena are not so altogether singular
That I could not think of non-metallic materials
Which are specially suited to join with one another.
Only lime, for example, will hold stones together;
Glue made of bull's flesh sticks wood so fast
That the pieces will often crack along the grain
Before the glue can be persuaded to relax its hold.
The juice of the grape mixes freely with spring water
While pitch is too heavy and oil too light to do so.
Purple dye from shellfish unites so closely with wool
That it is impossible to get it out,
Not if you were to let the waves beat upon it
— A whole sea would not be enough to wash it out.
There is only one substance which will fasten gold to gold
And will anything except tin serve to solder brass?
How many other examples I could produce!
No need to waste time by long-windedness;
It is not necessary to linger on a subject
Which I can sum up in a very few words.
Things of which the textures correspond with one another
So that the hollows of one fit the projections of the other,
Fit one another best and form the closest unions.
There are also things which fit like hooks and eyes
And hold themselves together in that way:
This seems to be the case with iron and the magnet.

Now I will explain how diseases are caused.
Where does it come from, this morbid force which can blow
Disaster together to strike at people and cattle?
The elements of many things, I have shown already,
Are beneficial and needed to keep life going:
But there must be many others flying about
Which bring death and disease. When many of these
Have by chance collected, the air itself will sicken.

205

All this force of sickness, all this pestilence,
Comes either from outside as clouds and mists
Come down through the sky, or else rises out of the ground
When it is wet and putrefies at a time
Of unseasonable rains combined with a blazing sun.

Have you noticed how people far from their homes and
                                                    countries
Are affected by the change in weather and water
And how unlike these may be in different places?
What a difference between the sky they have in Britain
And that in Egypt where the earth slopes down!
Or between Pontus and Gades, and so till you reach
The black races which have been baked in the sun!
We see four climates as different from each other
As the four winds and the quarters of the sky;
There are also men who differ in colour and looks
And diseases which attack the different races.

There is elephant disease which is generated
On the banks of the Nile in Egypt, and nowhere else.
In Attica it is feet which are affected,
In Achaea eyes; so different places are harmful
To different parts of the body: it is a matter of air.
As soon as a sort of weather that does not suit us
Is put in motion and a hurtful air creeps out
Like mist and cloud, it upsets all in its course
And, bringing change, when at last it reaches our climate
It makes our air like itself and so turns it against us.

Then suddenly there is disaster and pestilence.
It falls on the water or else attacks the crops
Or other food or fodder of men and beasts:
Or else its power hangs in the air
And when in breathing we draw in this air
The disease itself is inevitably taken in.
It is the same with diseases which overtake
Cattle or cause the flocks of sheep to sicken.
It makes no difference whether we go to places
Which do not suit us, and so change the sky which cloaks us,
Or whether the noxious atmosphere comes to us;
Or something else comes we are not accustomed to
Which can affect us when it reaches us first.

This sort of disease came like a tide of death
Carrying disaster over the Athenian fields,
Made roads deserted and emptied the city of people.
Coming from deep within Egypt where it arose,
Travelling far through the air over swimming fields,
It came to rest upon the people of Pandion
So they went down in troops to disease and death.
The first symptom was a burning in the head
And both eyes swimming in a red light.
The throat, blackened inside, would sweat with blood,
The way the voice should have come was choked with
                                        ulcers,
The tongue, which should speak for the mind, was
                             bleeding and clotted,
Weakened with pain, heavy in movement, rough to the
                                   touch.
Then through the throat the disease went on to the chest
And flowed into the sad heart of the sufferer;
Then all that kept life in would seem to give way.
Out of the mouth there came a fetid odour
Like that which comes from a corpse thrown out and
                                   rotting;
Then all the strength of the mind went and the body
Languished already on the threshold of death.
Unbearable pains were followed by fearful choking
And they complained and moaned as far as they could;
Night and day there were recurrent spasms
Shaking the muscles and the whole organism,
Breaking and wearying men already exhausted.
Yet nobody's skin seemed to be burning unduly,
If you touched it with the hands it seemed rather tepid;
But at the same time there were ulcers all over the body
Which looked inflamed as if burnt with the holy fire.
And the inner parts were in flames to the very bones;
A flame blazed in the stomach as in a furnace.
There was nothing so light or thin that it soothed the body,
Only wind and cold: some plunged their burning limbs
Into icy rivers or naked into the sea;
Many threw themselves headlong into wells
And arrived at the water with their mouths hanging open.
An insatiable thirst drowning their arid bodies
Made them think a deluge nothing but a few drops.

There was no respite from pain: their bodies lay fainting,
The doctors muttered and did not know what to say:
They were frightened of so many open, burning eyes
Turning towards them because they could not sleep.
There were many other signs of approaching death;
There were minds disturbed with suffering and fear,
Sad brows, faces which had grown furious and sharp,
Ears into which some sound was always drumming;
The breathing was quick or else deep and hesitant;
A shining torrent of sweat over the neck,
Spittle thin and tiny, of a yellowish colour,
Salty, and scarcely brought up by the hoarse cough.
The sinews of hands contracted, the whole body trembled;
From the feet upwards the cold began to creep
And could not be stopped: at the last moment the nostrils
Grew pinched and the point of the nose was sharp and thin;
The eyes were hollowed, the brow hollow; the skin was cold,
Hard, the mouth grimaced, the tense brow stood out.
It was not long before they died and stiffened;
As dawn began to break on the eighth day
Or perhaps the ninth, they parted with their lives.
If any (as some did) escaped from death
It was with foul ulcers and black diarrhoea
And after a little while consumption and death;
Or, with pains in the head, corrupted blood
Would flow continually from the choked nostrils;
And so the body itself would flow away.
If anyone escaped the discharge of nauseous blood
The disease went into his sinews and his joints
And finally the sexual organs themselves.
Some, afraid of crossing the threshold of death,
Survived by taking a knife to their sexual parts;
Some remained alive but lost both hands and feet,
With others it was the eyes which had to go;
To such an extent were they afraid of death.
And some of them were so taken with forgetfulness
That they could not even remember their own names.
Unburied bodies lay one on top of another
Yet the birds and wild beasts kept themselves at a distance
Because of the stench, or tasted the meat and died.
There was hardly a bird to be seen at all in those days
And the sullen animals would not come out of the forest;

Many of them took the foul disease and died.
The dogs who were faithful were the first to go,
They lay in the streets everywhere, panting and dying
As if the disease was twisting life out of their bodies.
Unaccompanied funerals hurried from every corner.
No remedy could be trusted; if there was anything
Which served to keep one breathing and watching the sky
It was sure to be the way out to death for others.
What was most pitiful in this calamity
Was that as soon as anyone saw himself touched
By the disease he considered himself condemned;
Failing at once he prostrated himself without courage,
Seeing his funeral, and gave up his breath on the spot.
There had indeed to be funeral after funeral;
At no time did the contagion of the plague
Cease to lay hands on one person after another
As if it were passing cattle or sheep through a gate.
Those who refused to face the sick in their households,
Caring too much for life and afraid of death,
Were soon punished by dying shamefully
In pain, deserted, helpless and disregarded.
Those who stayed near at hand died from contagion
And the tasks which they had been forced to undertake
By shame, or by gentle or complaining voices.
So that was how the best of them ended their days.

      ·   ·   ·   ·   ·

One upon the other, as they struggled to bury the crowd
Of their dead, they came back worn out with tears
And many of them took to their beds in grief.
At such a time there was no one unaffected,
If not by plague or death then at least by mourning.
Even the shepherds and the cattlemen
And the tough boys who usually follow the plough
Fell sick and shoved together in a hut,
Found death in poverty as well as disease.
On top of the lifeless children you could see
Lifeless parents, and sometimes on mothers and fathers
Children on the point of giving up life.
In no small part the plague came flowing in
From the fields to the town, brought in by the country
                                           people
Making their way from all sides as they sickened.

They filled all the houses and all the public places
And the concentrated infection left them in heaps.
Many, prostrated by thirst, crawled through the streets
And lay down by the Silenus heads at the fountain
Only to choke on finding so much sweet water.
You would see many others as they went through the streets,
Their limbs drooping against their half-dead bodies,
Stinking, in rags, dying in their own filth:
Nothing but skin and bones, and with their ulcers
And the muck that came from them almost buried already.

As for the holy sanctuaries of the gods,
Death had filled them up with corpses. Everywhere
The temples of the divinities were piled with bodies,
The guardians having filled them with their guests.
Neither the worship of the gods nor the gods themselves
Mattered any more: the present pain was enough.
Nobody thought any more of the ancient rites
Which had been observed in the city when people were
                                                    buried.
All was confusion and perturbation and everyone
Buried the corpse on his hands as best he could.
Poverty and necessity are persuasive.
Some people would push the bodies of their family
On to funeral piles intended for someone else
And set a light to them, all this with shouts
And bloody scuffles before they abandoned the bodies.

FyfieldBooks

Two millennia of essential classics

The extensive FyfieldBooks list includes

For more information, including a full list of Fyfield*Books* and a contents list for each title, and details of how to order the books in the UK, visit the Fyfield website at www.fyfieldbooks.co.uk or email info@fyfieldbooks.co.uk. For information about Fyfield*Books* available in the United States and Canada, visit the Routledge website at www.routledge-ny.com.